SINGLE MOTHERS SYNDROME
By Choice or By Design
(An Open Dialogue)

By
Dr. Brenda Brown, PhD
Educator & Best-Selling Author

Copyright © 2022 by Dr Brenda Brown, PhD

**Single Mothers Syndrome | By Choice or By Design
(An Open Dialogue)
Dr. Brenda Brown, PhD**
ISBN 9780578353494
ISBN 9780578353500 (e-book)

All rights reserved. No part of this publication may be reproduced, distributed or transmitted in any form or by any means, without prior written permission. Contact the publisher at bbrown9836@gmail.com.

Publisher's Note: This is a work of fiction. Names, characters, places, and incidents are a product of the author's imagination. Locales and public names are sometimes used for atmospheric purposes. Any resemblance to actual people, living or dead, or to businesses, companies, events, institutions, or locales is completely coincidental.

Book Layout © 2017 BookDesignTemplates.com
Cover Design by Will Martin Designs
Cover Photo by Inspirational Light Enterprise (ILE)
Inside Photo by JC Penny Studio
Hair by Whitney Brown and Britany Thomas
Vintage Color Block Coat from Dangerous Lee Mall
Copyeditor: Darla Nagel

Dialogue portions are used with permission of the participants.

Printed in the United States of America
By IngramSpark

The author is not responsible for websites (or their contents) that are not owned by the author.

DEDICATION

I dedicate this book to my children (Nathaniel, Britany, and Whitney), for letting me experience the kind of love that all parents wish for from their children; to my mother (Marchel) and my sisters and brothers (Marcella, Linda, Mary, James Dwight, Bryant Keith, James R., Lee, Eddie, and Ricky) for your endless and unwavering support. And, to all single mothers who are surviving the challenges of single parenting.

IN LOVING MEMORY

In memory of my father (Jim), and brothers (James Clifford, William Frederick, and Wayne Bikel).

ACKNOWLEDGMENT

I would like to recognize the 16 single mothers, from across the country, who shared their journey in hopes of inspiring, motivating, and provoking objective thought on single motherhood. Your input helped make this book a success. (Note: one mother is not listed per her request.)

Leigh Langston	Brandi A. Johnson
Bianca James	Whitney DL Brown
Kelcy Williams	Kimberley Ogburn
Veronica Moore	Reva Winningham
Sierra Wineman	Michell Berkley
Shareatha Brown-Person	Dr. Dawn Demps
Alexis Brown	Michelle Larde
Torri Gunter	

CONTENTS

Introduction	9
Life Isn't Supposed to Be This Way!	1
If It Doesn't Challenge You, It Won't Change You!	9
Life Doesn't Have to Be Perfect to Be Great!	13
Message from The Author	135
Single Mothers Ministry in the Church	137
Family Fusion: Single Parent, Value Yourself	147
The Saga of Single Parenting	155
Single Parenting: Questions Your Child May Ask and How to Answer Them	161
FAQ's & Resources	171
Bibliography	175
About the Contributors	177
Leigh "Dangerous Lee" Langston	178
Bianca "BJay" James	183
Kelcy Williams	185
Varonica Moore	187
Sierra Wineman	189
Alexis Rae Brown	191
Shareatha Brown-Person	193
Torri J. Gunter	195
Brandi Allicia Johnson	196

Whitney DL Brown...198
Kimberley D. Ogburn, M.A. LPCC 199
Reva Caughel Winningham 201
Michell Berkley..202
Dr. Dawn Demps..204
About the Author 209
Dr. Brenda Brown..209
Media Articles..213
Social Media 213
Books by Dr. Brenda Brown...................................215
Notes 218

Introduction

As a society, we have a tendency to place labels on each other in order to categorize groups of people. Oftentimes, your relationship status, single or married, carries a lot of significance and weight. The classification of being married, instead of single, signifies something different in social and legal settings. The classifications also carry different psychological implications. When children are involved, these classification labels go even further and carry a different weight.

      Regardless of our relationship status, as mothers, we are all one! However, being a single mother comes with its own set of rules and stressors. Society would have you believing that as a single mother you have failed at building a "normal" family structure that included a mother and a father. Society's other implication for single mothers is that our family unit will be one of unhappiness and be "broken" because of the absence of a father. Undeniably, as single mothers by choice, we are going against society's norms in having and raising our children out of wedlock.

Unfortunately, these negative connotations and implications that society puts on single motherhood, like it is something bad or undesirable, leads us farther away from the truth that we are mothers first and single second. This subtle psychological viewpoint of looking down on the single mother creates a feeling of separateness.

We all can acknowledge that it is hard to be a single mother. Even with the assistance state government offers, single parenting is still hard. As single mothers, we are not supported or acknowledged in a socially inclusive and psychologically supportive way. Because of the "separate" label, we are expected to be strong and raise our kids as best we can, on our own.

But we are not entirely on our own. We can gain support from the experiences of single mothers and from the resources in the pages of this book.

CHAPTER ONE

Life Isn't Supposed to Be This Way!

Single parenting is challenging! I think many of us can relate and say life isn't supposed to be this way, but we find ourselves asking the question "Where do we go from here?" (TerKeurst, 2018).

As a little girl, I did not dream of becoming a single mother who would struggle to make ends meet and raise my children on my own. When life was challenging, I never used the phrase of "I'm a single mother," as if it were a disease or disability, with the expectation that society was to take care of me. I had to figure out what to do in order to meet the expectations I had established for my children and myself. And, I did it!

Yes, as a young single mother, there was a subtle implication, made by some, that I had failed at building the dream that society created and shared of the "stereotypical American family - two parents and one or more children, with a father who worked outside the home and a mother who stayed home and cared for the children and the household" (American Academy of Pediatrics, 2015), with everyone living happily as a normal family unit and creating dreams together. I would not be where I am at today, if I had allowed thoughts of how others looked down on me as a single mother, like being one was something bad or undesirable, into my mind. While I did not set out to be a single mother, I was determined to be the best mother I could. I built my happy family.

According to the American Academy of Pediatrics, 30% of American families were headed by single parents in 2015, whether divorced, widowed, or never married. Some children lived in foster families, in stepfamilies, or in gay or lesbian families. Both parents worked outside the home in more than two-thirds of families (American Academy of Pediatrics, 2015).

Today, with the entry of so many more women into the workforce, with the increasing divorce rate, and with the growing number of single-parent households, other family structures have become more common. Your child will have friends who live in households with different structures. Families are important to children and they are trying to understand two things about families: "the different structures that families can take and the changes in structure, lifestyles and relationships that can occur" (American Academy of Pediatrics, 2015). You can expect your child to ask questions about why people get divorced, why mothers and fathers don't live together, where their father is, and why he is not in the home. If we want to build strong and healthy children, we need to be prepared to answer these kinds of questions with more than mere slogans or quick replies (American Academy of Pediatrics, 2015). Your child should never see the hatred you may have for the father, especially when you are responding to your child's questions.

I will not pretend being a single mother was easy. There were great burdens I remember facing as a single mother. Two of them, as echoed in the words of single mother Missy Robinson (2014), were "the overwhelming sense of responsibility for my time, energy and resources" and "the isolation of carrying that burden alone." I didn't have a husband to tag in, to remove my self-doubt, to help make decisions, or to alleviate anxiety about money (the lack of it). I don't even need to mention the many sleepless nights. I had to earn the rent, provide the groceries, prepare the meals, teach the manners, instill godly values, oversee schooling, develop a social life, etc. Without my faith and support system, I wouldn't have made it. As a single parent, you do not have to raise your children alone. Ask for support from your immediate family, cousins, or friends or from a colleague. Check to see if there are single-parent support groups in your community or online. If you want strong and healthy children, you must take care of yourself first. Your support system can watch your children for a few hours so that you can have some me time.

As hard as it was, it wasn't impossible! As a single mother, my first priority was my children. Earlier, I mentioned that I had expectations for my children and myself. I taught my children, by example, how to be hard workers, how to reach for their own stars, how to write their own story, and how not to accept someone's no when yes was the obvious choice for them. I worked hard at showing them how to be leaders and not followers, how to be critical thinkers and not just thinkers. I taught them how to color outside the lines.

As a single mother, I didn't give up on myself. I earned my associate's, bachelor's, master's, and then doctoral degree. I worked and retired, after 26 years, from Baker College as an administrator and adjunct faculty member. I held the same high expectations for my children, whom I, by example, inspired to achieve higher education degrees. Beyond home and work, I also believed in giving back to my community. I volunteered with many local nonprofit programs. I did all this as a single mother. Again, as hard as it was, it wasn't impossible! I relied heavily on my faith and support system. Mary McLeod Bethune said, "Without faith, nothing is possible. With it, nothing is impossible."

I didn't allow society to put me in a category of inferiority. I did not allow myself to become victimized. I did not use the statement of "I'm a single mother" as an excuse, or justification, or reason to hold back. I'm encouraging all single mothers who use this statement in holding back from your full potential to please stop. It is a disservice to your children and to yourself. Where is your faith?

Now, I'm sure some of the married women who are reading this are probably thinking, "I know what it feels like to be a single mother," or "I feel like a single mom," because your husband is away working all the time. In response, I say that there is a distinction between married women and single women raising children. If you have a husband who provides and/or supplements your income, a home, healthcare, or even a contribution toward your decision-making and family direction, I really don't think you get it or know how we feel. It's tough and isolating in a way you cannot imagine.

CHAPTER TWO

If It Doesn't Challenge You, It Won't Change You!

Single mother syndrome is when single mothers dwell on the negative thoughts and beliefs society has concerning them. It is when we make a conscious decision to give up on ourselves and our children. It is when society tells us that we are alone and we believe it. It is when society tells us we have to struggle to get by because we don't have what the rest of the country has. It is when society tells us that two-parent households are doing so much better than those of us who are doing it solo. It is when we start believing that we have to be super-strong warrior-mothers who can and will raise our children on our own. It is when we shun the idea of help, or at least have a hard time accepting it if offered.

This type of thinking leads to some single mothers taking on a victim role. We begin to characterize single motherhood as a particular abnormality or condition. We convince ourselves that we are strong enough to do it on our own and so present to the world this tough outer shell that does not allow anyone in. This creates more separation. We all need help from one another sometimes. Being open to it is key.

I am sure that we all can relate to having used the excuse that "I am a single mom" on a few occasions. I used to tell myself I couldn't do something or to try to play the victim role to get sympathy. I was 23 years old and had just given birth to my son 2 days after graduation from college. I had no job prospects and was totally dependent on my parents. I was embarrassed and ashamed. I returned home with a bachelor's degree, a newborn baby, the stigma attached to having a child out of wedlock, and the ultimate embarrassment of my child's father kicking me and our son to the curb soon after he was drafted by the NFL. I soon realized there was no need at all to feel embarrassed. I also realized that in order to get out of the single mother syndrome mindset, I would have to begin to look differently at society's definition of family and do something. Remember what I wrote earlier on how other family structures have become more common.

I chose to do something different. It wasn't easy, but I did it. I broke out of the mindset of single mother syndrome and refused to be a victim. I took advantage of the opportunities to reach out to my family and others for support and resources. I applied for food stamps. I got my first job. I furthered my education. I volunteered in my community. I created awesome and inspiring journeys for my children. I opened up and expanded myself without a partner. I built a solid foundation for my children that fostered stability and a welcoming home. I went beyond the definitions and labels. My mindset was "I am enough to make it happen.

CHAPTER THREE

Life Doesn't Have to Be Perfect to Be Great!

We all have our personal bias toward and perceptions of single mothers. This chapter shares the views and firsthand experiences of 16 single mothers and the steps they took in adjusting to the pressures of single parenting. The 16 participants represent eight states: Alabama, Arizona, Georgia, Indiana, Michigan, Mississippi, Nevada, and Ohio. Each contributor completed a 29-question survey on the negative labels and connotations that society places on single mothers, as well as their thoughts on:

1. As a single mother, what gave you inner strength from day to day
2. Who are the people who made up your support system? How involved were they?
3. As single mothers, are we our worst enemy? Explain your answer.
4. Describe your typical weekday.
5. Why does society have such a negative view of single mothers?
6. What sacrifices, if any, when kids come first, did you make?
7. What are some quality things you do or can do with your kids?
8. What personal advice do you have for mothers who would rather be their child's friend instead of their child's parent?
9. How do you make it on your budget?
10. What or who inspired you to not give up as a single mother?
11. How did you maintain the perfect balance?
12. What is your secret to success?

13. How do you respond to people who ask nosy questions, such as (a.) Where is your child's father? (b.) Does the father see your child often? (c.) Does the father pay child support? (d.) Do you get any kind of state assistance? (e.) What name is on your child's birth certificate?
14. As a single mother, do you have any regrets?
15. When is it the right time for you to date?
16. What are some essential qualities for a potential mate?
17. What are some essential qualities for a potential mate?
18. What are your thoughts on live-in boyfriends?
19. Describe how overworked or overwhelmed you are from day to day.
20. Did you have a co-parenting plan that worked? If yes, what does it look like? If no, are you interested in having a co-parenting plan?

21. What strengths do you possess that enhanced your role as a single mother?
22. Were you logistically (i.e., had living space for your child, could take a leave of absence from work, had childcare arrangements, etc.) prepared to become a single mother?
23. How did you handle the stress and pressure of single parenting?
24. What calms you?
25. What is your occupation?
26. What was the most difficult part of being a single mother?
27. What is your favorite part about being a single mother?
28. Do you attend single-parent support groups where you live? If yes, how effective are they? If not, would you be interested in receiving information about single-parent support groups?
29. Additional comments and/or suggestions

Questions & Answers

As a single mother, what gave you inner strength from day to day

1. My faith and being there for my sons.
2. Knowing I have two beautiful kids that look up to me.
3. Seeing the face of the little human who depended on me to work hard and be great. Don't get me wrong, I have had days where I have been in tears and suffered a great deal of heartache. After feeling down and out, I'd pray to God for the strength needed to provide for my child(ren).
4. My strength came from my family and my financial stability to care for my son.
5. My faith and a great support system.
6. Knowing that my daughter depends on me is my strength to get through from day to day. She depends on me to take care of her needs and also wants.
7. The single greatest motivating factor for me is love of my children. Due to that love, I am

committed to making sure they are not limited in life in terms of resources or opportunities because they come from a "single mother" household.
8. Knowing that I had to make a better life for my children.
9. Knowing that I have two children that are depending on me that have a father who chooses when he wants to deal with them. So, I said with or without him, I have to make sure they are wanting for nothing.
10. Love for my child and my responsibility to be a mother.
11. God gave me the strength to continue as a single mother raising my son in Indianapolis, IN, with no family in the same state.
12. My relationship with God and prayer, my family and my desire to survive.
13. My inner strength comes with the love and joy that I have for my children. I have always been a "go-getter," curious about the world and ways to experience my immediate

surroundings and different places away from what I know to be familiar. I have shared this same vision/experience with my children from their toddler ages, and throughout each milestone. Every time I witnessed such growth in their different experiences of each child, I would work harder at providing new experiences for them.

14. As a single mother what gave me Inner Strength is knowing that my girls were depending on me. Knowing that I must set an example for them. And the thought of always feeling blessed.

15. My own self-love and determination to be a loving mother to my child.

16. My children gave me the inner strength to succeed. I had a child during an era when it was heavily frowned upon when having a child out of wedlock. I was determined to show the world that being single with a child would not deter me.

As a single mother, what gave you inner strength from day to day

Your Thoughts

Who are the people who made up your support system? How involved were they?

1. My strongest support was from my church family. I had two friends that were always there when I needed them. They were mostly sounding boards for when I was frustrated or upset.
2. My parents, my grandmother, the father's parents. All are very involved.
3. With my daughter my support system was my Mom, Dad, Maternal Grandparents, my best friend and her Paternal Great Aunt and cousins. When I had my son my Maternal Great Aunt and Great Uncle stepped in and helped me out tremendously after my Granny requested a strong male presence. My Granny passed away the same week she had that conversation with them. My son has not ever wanted for anything. I am forever grateful for that.
4. Family and Aunt Linda who kept my only son instead of him going to daycare initially. Most

first-time moms have severe "daycare anxiety"!
5. Their dad, grandmothers and aunts (maternal and paternal). All are very involved.
6. My family is def my support system. My parents, stepparents, and my brother help me out so much. They keep my daughter for me while I am away at work. Without them I wouldn't be able to be where I'm at, and I am forever grateful for them.
7. My children's fathers are involved. I also have the assistance of my children's grandparents and my own siblings. In terms of the fathers— I have critiques, especially from early on, but no parent is perfect. The co-parenting relationship with both of my children's fathers has evolved for the better. Ultimately, my kids know they have fathers who will be there for them and that is what is most important.
8. My aunt and my neighbor
9. Their Aunt Betty (dad's side). She keeps them whenever needed since they were 6 weeks old.

My mom lives in Auburn Hills and she will have them come down time to time on the weekends to stay with her. Also, my best friend, Quiesha, who will get them to and from school for me when I needed her to.

10. My mother and grandmother were a great help to me. They often babysat, bought clothing for my daughter, and most importantly gave love.
11. My grandmother and mother were my support system that helped me with my son. When school was out for the summer he stayed in Michigan.
12. My entire family, especially my sister who lives near me. She assisted any way possible. When my dad was living, he played a major role in assisting with my children every single day.
13. I must add that I had a terrific support system. My maternal grandmother helped me a great deal as well as my middle sister with babysitting as I attended college classes as well as working.

14. My only support was my dad who lived in another state five states away. We spoke weekly on phone.
15. My mother and siblings. They all were supportive emotionally. I lived with my mother until my first child was 6 years old. I did not qualify for state assistance, so they all helped me with housing, food and clothing. While I worked, she made sure he got on and off the bus. My brothers provided male bonding time by taking him places and playing sports with him.

Who are the people who made up your support system? How involved were they?

As single mothers, are we our worst enemy? Explain your answer.

1. No, I don't think so. We are strong and independent. We are resourceful, good at time management, and financially creative.
2. I beat myself up every day about the way things turned out.
3. As a single mother we can be our own worst enemy, well if you are a responsible parent. You want the best for your child. To this day I still criticize myself at times for not thinking a plan through in its entirety, i.e. moving, purchasing property, schools, career choices.
4. Some are...depends on three factors: family support, financial stability, and self-worth.
5. Sometimes. I think we put the pressure of being perfect on ourselves to prove to others we can be great mothers without being married, when reality is most people don't think that about us. Especially our children.
6. I believe that we are. There are so many shoes and positions we try to fill. I think we believe

that we have to be if not perfect, close to it or our kids will not turn out the way we hope that they will.

7. I think everyone, single mother or otherwise, is their own "worst enemy." This is why an honest, trustworthy and strong tribe is needed around you to hold up the mirror to your life. As a Black single mother, I do believe we are heavily castigated, stereotyped and deemed the bane of Black existence. We must be mindful not to fall into that line of thinking about ourselves and our peer single mothers.

8. That's hard to say! 'Cause as a single mother we might put more on ourselves. We often forget that it takes a village.

9. We as single mothers could get very stressed and worry about a lot of different things. We don't give ourselves that "me" time that we need.

10. Speaking for myself, I definitely am not my own worst enemy as a single mother. I do not make choices that cause problems in my life.

11. I don't believe so. Sometimes it may seem like it because we try and do everything ourselves without bothering others. But for the most part I would have to say no.

12. I believe that as a single mother we may at times feel that we're not doing enough or we may blame ourselves for missing certain events that our child/children would like for us [to] attend or just having too busy of a schedule that we may feel that we're not always emotionally present because of our daily schedules.

13. No, but we single mothers feel pressure to be perfect, or we overcompensate for absent or abusive, deadbeat fathers

14. Sometimes we can be our worst enemy. Being a single mother does not negate us from assuming our responsibility to raise our children. Throughout my teaching career, I recall single mothers saying, "But, I'm a single mother" to justify why they didn't submit an assignment or study for an exam. I would then

share my experiences as a single mother raising young children. We [the student and I] would devise a time management plan that showed them how to get things done. We worked on finding support systems to help.

As single mothers, are we our worst enemy? Explain your answer.

Your Thoughts

Describe your typical weekday.

1. Up at 5:30 am to shower and dress. 6:30 am wake up the boys, cook breakfast and make sure they have everything they need for school. Get them out the door and I am at work by 7:30 am. Work until 4:30. Pick up the boys from the sitter, cook supper and supervise homework. Eat supper, clean up and watch some TV before getting the boys in bed. I was in bed about 10:00.

2. Wake up, feed my children, playtime, doing educational activities, lunch, nap time, play, dinner, baths, bedtime

3. Prior to Covid-19 a typical weekday would be...my alarm goes off at 6:00 am, I would wake my son up to get him ready to catch the bus, he'd brush his teeth, get dressed, I'd make lunch that morning and a peanut butter sandwich for him to eat while waiting on the bus. He's a picky eater. I'd go back to the house wake my daughter up. She's old enough to get herself together. I'd get showered and

ready for work. I would drive my daughter two blocks to her bus stop then I would head to work. I would work my 9-5, as I was late most days. My son would have to attend an after-school program due to my work schedule, so I would pick him up, my daughter would be home before me. I'd cook (only 3 days out of the week), help with homework. Then it is time for showers and bed.
4. A 7-to-4 career and then homework as well as realistic valuable conversations with my son. How do you see the world you live in?
5. My children live with their dad in another city, an hour away. My day to day is usually consumed by phone calls, text and cash apps. When my visitation days come, it gets a little hectic meeting their dad or getting to the city.
6. I am gone anywhere from 3-5 days at a time, and also home for that same amount. While I'm home, I make sure breakfast is made in the morning, then I take my daughter to school. While she is there, sometimes, I go up to the

school and have lunch with her. If not, I'm usually just running errands and taking care of things around the house. Once school is out, I'll pick her up and we try to go to a park or play outside. We do homework, shower, relax, then go to bed.

7. Get up, shower. Get kids up, fix breakfast. Feed, make sure they get dressed, clean the house, fix lunch, feed the kids, watch my stories while I check on the kids, start dinner, feed kids, clean the kitchen, play with the kids, then make sure they take their baths. Put to bed then pick up toys and books then take a shower and go to bed.

8. Monday will be a late start for all of us so after I get them on the bus off to school at 7:40 am, I'll go back home, get dressed and head off to work by 9:00 am until 5:00 pm. Get home, cook dinner, do homework. The rest of the week they have to be on the bus by 6:40 am and I will leave maybe 30 minutes to lay down before I have to be up to be at work at 8:30 am,

which I will get off earlier most days through the week to get them from the bus stop 'cause I was nervous about them continuously crossing ML King. Fridays when I got off, we will go out and hang out at P3, the valley, movies or our favorite store, Wal-Mart. If I don't have to work the weekend, we will attend church on Sundays, then get laundry done and get ready to do it all over again.

9. A typical weekday prior to the coronavirus was getting up early to take my daughter to school, then I'd come home and perhaps go back to sleep for a short while before I had to be to work. After work I'd pick my daughter up from school or run her to an event or extracurricular activity. If she didn't have anything after school, we'd head home and I'd cook dinner. The rest of the night would be us doing our own thing and coming together to talk and watch television.

10. (1) Dress for work and my son for school. (2) Make breakfast. (3) Dropped my son off at

daycare. (4) Worked 8 hours a day. (5) Pick up son from daycare. (6) Cooked dinner for me and my son. (7) If my son had homework, I made sure it was complete in grade school. (8) Went to bed.

11. Prayer, work, household duties including cooking, cleaning etc., writing and other outside work activities I participate in. Weekly Bible class. Activities pertaining to my children.

12. A typical weekday involves working, grocery and clothes shopping; checking my children's school assignments and making sure the assignments are completed; cooking; this including laundry and house chores in general with the help of my two adolescents. When all three of my children were small my schedule was very busy as I was attending college, participating in internships, homework, working, and play activities with my children.

13. My typical weekend is like any other day. I'm usually working, cleaning and taking care of the girls.
14. I worked an 8-hour day. Then go to daycare to pick up my son. Go home, cook, care for him, love him, clean my house, finish my master's level 20, or 10-page papers or study. I then go to bed at 11 pm or midnight. I wake up at 6 am and start all over. I did this for two years when my son was a baby.
15. I am a grandmother who is helping my daughter with her children while she is working and in college. My typical workday is getting up before my grands, sipping on a cup of coffee, do my daily devotional, and map out my day. Once the girls wake up, I feed them breakfast and allow them playtime. Then I plan a structure activity. Because we are in the middle of a pandemic [COVID-19], I help my granddaughter with her virtual schooling. I pretty much do not have free time to myself until the girls are down for a nap. Then, I try

to get a load of clothes washed, catch up on my emails or do other work on computer. Once the girls wake up, we go outside to play.

Describe your typical weekday

Your Thoughts

Why does society have such a negative view of single mothers?

1. Judgmental assumptions. They have no idea why the mom is single but assume they were "loose women." My heart breaks for the moms who lost their spouse but are still judged without mercy.
2. Because they don't know what it's really like to be in that situation
3. There are a lot of single mothers out in the world who are not responsible, and don't want to care for their children. Unfortunately, the negative view is placed on all single mothers and not just the bad mothers.
4. Because it has become the new norm with sometimes massive consequences that spiral children downward and with little self-control. They are angry and deprived. Statistical data shows that most will not be successful if no support system.
5. From my personal experience, the negativity is geared more towards single women than

single mothers. Those that I have encountered that do show negativity towards single mothers specifically, it's based off of traditional and sometimes religious perspectives, and also double standards. Women are supposed to be married when they have children but men don't have to be. Women with children by more than one father are viewed as "loose" even if she was married when her children were conceived. Men often get praised if they have multiple children with different women.

6. I believe in the African American society; a lot of people see single mothers just as "baby mommas" and we are so much more than that. There is a thought that there is something wrong with the mother, whether it is that she is emotionally unstable, or that she was promiscuous. Or that she had a child to keep the individual around for emotional and financial reasons.

7. First off because we are women. Then we have the audacity to be women without collars—collars being a man to keep us reined in. This is tied into the assumed promiscuity of single mothers. Then if a single mother is able to raise up her children successfully—however we define that—her situation is touted as the exception or she becomes a threat to the narrative that without a man in the home, the woman and her child will be a failure. Our status as women makes us safe and acceptable scapegoats to all that is wrong in society without examining issues of education, employment, incarceration, poverty, gender, racism and other equity issues.

8. I feel that society may have a negative view because to some, single mothers equal irresponsibility. Single mothers are often stereotyped to be uneducated, poor decision makers that may not have support. It's far from the truth but I feel that we are viewed in this

manner without knowing our individual situations.

9. They feel as if they depend on the state more than anything, which may be true in some cases, especially if they are not getting assistance from the father.
10. Society often sees single mothers as whores or just all-around bad decision makers and I think that has to do with religious beliefs, racism, and classism.
11. You should be married before you have kids.
12. I believe society has a belief that single mothers are "lazy," undereducated, on welfare, and little to no life goals. Of course, such belief is totally false.
13. I believe society has a negative view of single mothers because they are unwed mothers. Most believe them to be s**** or worse.
14. I have no idea, bias bigotry, I guess. Single mothers are superheroes!
15. I think that society bases their negative views on single mothers because there are some

mothers who, instead of working, prefer to continue to have children so that the system can take care of them. You have some mothers who totally neglect their children when it comes to caring, nurturing, and taking care of their child's basic needs. Society doesn't compliment single mothers who are holding down the fort. Instead they criticize our single mothers who are neglectful.

Why does society have such a negative view of single mothers?

Your Thoughts

What sacrifices, if any, when kids come first, did you make?

1. I rarely dated and never had men at the house. The boys always came first, emotionally and financially
2. Going out with friends, and partying, doing young adult things. I gave up everything to raise my kids and work to raise them and give them everything they need.
3. Not buying for myself but for them. Ensure they eat before I do. Paying bills before having (adult) fun. Overall, just making mature adult decisions. Kids did not ask to be here. I chose to keep them.
4. Putting my own thoughts and schema aside for my child...His emotional well-being comes first.
5. Where do I begin?? I went an entire year without buying myself any shoes or clothes to make sure my kids' extracurricular activity fees could be paid. I've moved to another city for my kid and also allowed my kids to move

to another city. That was extremely difficult to do. I've worked three jobs to make sure I could provide for them also.

6. As a younger single mother, it is the simple things such as hanging out with friends and going out on dates. I have to say no a lot to those things because I need to stay home and take care of my child.

7. My kids have been the inspiration for most of what is good in my life. They actually got me on the right path to where I am now, so I don't see any real sacrifices. Perhaps, I don't go out with friends or to poetry shows as often.

8. I put my life on hold. My children have always come first. I said when all my children were grown then it's my time to think of myself.

9. I don't really feel like I had to make any sacrifices. I've been able to do everything I've wanted to do over the years of being a single mom.

10. Since my family lived in another state, I had a lot of sacrifices when it came to my son...such as dating and going on trips with the girls.
11. I actually put my needs last. I was a part of any activities they were involved in. I came up with monies needed for their needs and some of their wants. I worked two jobs when needed to make ends meet. I helped them in all areas of their lives.
12. I wouldn't buy myself anything new for months at a time. I would at times turn down dates or hang out with my friends because I wanted to make sure my kids knew I was always by their side. I spent my money on my children. In general, there were more times than not where I would just go without because I wanted to make sure they were okay.
13. I've made all sacrifices when it comes to my kids from being the last to eat to not even eating. Sacrificing my hair and nails so that they can have those things done. I sacrifice

being in relationships just so they can help support financially.

14. Dating was off-limits when my son was young and I was in graduate school. My choice, my focus.
15. A personal life. After raising my children, I'm trying to get a personal life again.

What sacrifices, if any, when kids come first, did you make?

Your Thoughts

What are some quality things you do or can do with your kids?

1. We camped every summer. That was their favorite thing to do. We had bonfires, swam and just enjoyed life. We also went to lots of free events, and Back to the Bricks was a must. Flint Public Library offers so much.
2. Going for walks, reading, counting, letters, coloring, dancing, playing outside
3. Outdoor fun activities, watching movies, cooking, cleaning, homework
4. Tactical activities such as board games and music
5. I try not to miss any of their games or award ceremonies. I've always been that way. I know how it feels to not have anyone there to cheer or support you and I never wanted them to experience that. It's a little harder to do now that we live so far apart. However, I still make about 85% of their special moments.
6. When I am home, we love going to parks so we do that pretty frequently. When the weather

isn't that great, we go to trampoline parks or we stay home and sing and dance. We both love watching movies so we rent a lot of movies and eat popcorn, which she loves.

7. I do the same things two-parent households do I would assume: game nights, movies at home or at the theater, parks, bowling, roller-skating, trampoline parks.

8. With my children we read a lot, played games, and we sat around just talking.

9. We go to the library and read; go shopping; me and my daughter have mother daughter dates as well as mother son dates just to have small talk.

10. My daughter and I have talks, walks, go to dinner, shopping, movies, and concerts. I also support her in her future career endeavors by attending her shows/events and encouraging her with her future career plans.

11. My son is now 20 and in college. When he was a young child, we went to the park a lot and the YMCA because he loved to play baseball.

12. Pray, read the Bible, play games together, help them to fulfill the dreams
13. When my children were small I would always take them to the local playground and actively swing with them; slide down the sliding board with them; as well as taking them to the lake as well as local community swimming pools, going to the zoo, traveling and having them taste different foods on these traveling trips. I would also take them for car rides especially at night on summer days so they could look at the night lights, which was fun.
14. We do quality things such as just watching TV, playing games and making funny videos.
15. I always went to the pool with my son. He learned to swim first and learned to walk in the baby pool in our community. I was also able to make friends with other mothers, married and single.
16. Play outside with them. Read books. Have tea parties (if girls). Talk and listen to them.

What are some quality things you do or can do with your kids?

Your Thoughts

What personal advice do you have for mothers who would rather be their child's friend instead of their child's parent?

1. Give mom a break. Take the kids to events when reasonable, even if it's just an hour or two. Offer to teach them things that mom is not able to do. I asked for my boys to be mentored by our church, but it never happened. I taught them what I could about cars, fishing and all those "boy" things that a male role model should have done.
2. It's okay to be your child's friend but to a point, you still have to be the parent and not let your child get away with thinking you're just their friend.
3. Be a mother/parent first. The level of respect is different than being your child's friend. Be their friend when they become grown, secure and stable. And still be a parent first!
4. "The future belongs to those who prepare for it today!" (Malcolm X) Meaning instill value,

worth, and education in your child so that they can excel!

5. It's a very dangerous line to cross. Kids need structure, discipline and stability. It's hard to enforce those things when they don't have a certain level of respect and honestly healthy fear for you. It's OK to joke and have fun, but it should stop right there. They should never think that they are your equal.

6. PARENT FIRST. Growing up my mother, who was a single parent for a while, would say, "I am your parent, not your friend." I HATED when she said that. Ha-ha. But as one now I understand. I feel like if you try to be a friend first it's easier for the child to cross lines because they see you just as that...a friend, not a parent. It opens the door up that can potentially allow disrespect. I think you can be a parent and be open to conversations with your child that they may have with their friends.

7. I am not sure if I believe that to be an "either/or" situation. I am my children's

mother first and foremost, yet, I am also their friend. I have made a determined effort to not be dictatorial, especially as they get older, but guide my kids as they think through situations. I am trying to raise critical thinkers able to navigate life effectively on their own without needing someone to tell them what to do. Some level of friendship is necessary if I expect them to share parts of their life with me so I can help them think through things.

8. That is a big mistake.
9. It's okay to have a bond with your child so they can feel like they can talk to about anything and not hide nothing from you but at the end of the day, it's still a boundary of respect.
10. That's interesting because over the years I have told my daughter that I am not her friend, I am her mother, and that is more important than being a friend. I'm sure it may work for some mothers but I feel like being a friend first, especially when your child is not an adult

yet, is a recipe for disaster. When does the parenting come in?

11. The emotional role of the parent is built on love, affection, and esteem. It's an essential part of being a parent. But your role as a parent is not just emotional. And your child is not your friend.

12. Don't do it. Being a friend leaves the door wide open for your children. They have to have boundaries. Our goal is to keep them from the dangers in the world, and we must be a parent who can guide our children as opposed to a friend.

13. It's not a good choice at all as I've witnessed many times where the child feels like their parent's equal making for poor boundaries and enmeshed relationships.

14. I believe it's okay for your child to be able to come and talk to you as if you are one of their friends. They should be able to be open up to you but there should be some boundaries and level of respect. Me and my girls are very

close. I am their friend but they know that I am their mother first.

15. My advice is you are not your child's friend. You are the spiritual advisor and protector of your child. Period. My child doesn't ever have to like me, only to respect me!
16. Don't. You should be a parent first. Once they are adults, you can be their friend. But always remember, you are a parent first.

What personal advice do you have for mothers who would rather be their child's friend instead of their child's parent?

Your Thoughts

How do you make it on your budget?

1. Coupons, coupons and more coupons! I got the Sunday paper every week and planned meals around what was on sale. I shopped yard sales and thrift stores whenever possible.
2. Look at things as do I need this or want this, and will this be of use or not.
3. Oh honey, I haven't...It has truly been my downfall. I pray every month and God makes it happen.
4. Currently I am unemployed, so times get hard. When I get money, I send what I can. I always contribute to food for them and small things like haircuts and money for recreational things. When I was working, every paycheck I made sure that they were included in my bill budget as well as my recreational budget. The same dollar amounts each time. It helped to save and also prepare for their busy summers.
5. Family. I live at home currently so that helps me out financially a lot. There are places I would love to go to and things I'd love to buy

but I don't. I take care of my child's needs first and then go from there.

6. I put money in multiple places (accounts) that is pulled automatically from my paycheck, so I always have a little something somewhere. I try to make smart money moves, such as, I pay cash for my cars—so no car note. I am living on campus in family housing, so that is a huge money savings. I drive a Prius so I help save the planet and my pockets on gas. I have often kept more than one income—usually my main job and some side hustle, be it grant writing, cooking dinners or doing DoorDash.

7. It was hard but I made it work.

8. I make sure my bills are paid up a little ahead so if I came into a hardship, I wouldn't be in such a big bind. I sometimes have to explain to the kids that we don't have extra money to spend at the time if it's not a necessity.

9. That has been challenging as I am not and never have been financially stable. I suppose I

just don't spend money on things we don't need very often.

10. Sacrificing the things that I want and focusing on needs. Work a second job if necessary, to meet the needs.

11. It has been very challenging when you have more than one child and a budget that you're trying to stretch which includes yourself. I keep track of bills on my wall calendar of what's due each week/month. When it comes to including social activities, the month prior to certain events, I'm having to pay half of a bill instead of in full. As it relates to shopping for groceries, I will budget for foods that we eat more of and shop for items on sale. When buying clothes, I would schedule each child on different days of the month to help keep me within my budget.

12. That's very funny. I usually don't. And when I do it is far and in between. I generally don't buy name brand anymore for myself. I buy that for the girls.

13. I sacrificed a lot, didn't travel or buy a home till I was financially able to do so. Keep my childcare needs over adequate.
14. Barely. I was paycheck to paycheck. But I spent my money wisely on things that we needed. Rarely, did I buy my children things just because they wanted it versus need it. As my income increased, I found myself being able to do more for the kids. I remember being a student in college without a computer or WiFi. I couldn't afford either. I would take my kids with me to my job in the evenings or Saturdays so that I could use the computer/Wifii in order to complete my studies.

How do you make it on your budget?

What or who inspired you to not give up as a single mother?

1. My faith was the only thing that kept me going. No matter what, God provided everything my boys and I needed.
2. My mother and my grandmother have really helped me.
3. I have closed the door and given up several times. This just was not the way I envisioned my life. Several breaths later, a talk with God, my best friends seemed to help me pull it together. After all my broke best friends are counting on me.
4. My faith
5. My kids. Everything is always for them.
6. I guess I'd have to say my family. I grew up knowing that my parents sacrificed their dreams because they had a family at a young age. They always told me no matter what to follow my dreams. My aunts and uncles were the same way. We have a pretty close-knit family and they are willing to do just about

whatever they can to make sure my cousins and I get to our dream place.

7. My children were inspiration enough. They have been my greatest blessing.
8. Giving up was not an option. My children kept me going.
9. My mother and grandmother. My mother had me at 16 years old which my father wasn't never around but she did an AMAZING job on raising me with the help of my grandmother, who was a big help even though me and my kids' father were still together up until a few months before she passed March of 2010. She instills in me on how to be independent.
10. My mother was a single mother so I'm sure she was an influence, but giving up is not and never will be an option.
11. The love I have [for] my son inspired me not to give [up] on him.
12. My parents and my upbringing. Also, my pastor and family.

13. I have a strong family support whom has encouraged me throughout my motherhood experience. But I have always been my own cheerleader. I'm a strong-willed person. I believe in myself and giving my best efforts to my children so that mimics some of my motivation and drive of life experiences as well as builds their own vision of life experiences which inspires me.
14. The heavenly father inspired me, I inspired myself, and my mother inspired me.
15. My dad, and my male friends always encouraged me, and made me feel that I was a great mom to my son! My dad gave me great advice when I struggled with parenting decisions.
16. My mother was my inspiration. She raised me and my siblings by working two to three jobs. I had an absentee father.

What or who inspired you to not give up as a single mother?

Your Thoughts

How did you maintain the perfect balance?

1. Don't know that I ever had it.
2. Just staying positive!
3. When I lived closer to my support system, I had relief options. I have since moved 12 hours away from my support system. The kids are older, so if I have to step out for an hour or two, I can do so. In the summer months they return home and I can have a mental break for two months.
4. I am a well-rounded and idealistic mom.
5. I don't think I have. I do my best and pray that it's enough.
6. I try to leave work at work. When I'm home, I try to focus on my daughter and enjoy our time together.
7. There is no such thing as a perfect balance—only perfect harmony. I attend to the parts that need to be attended as situations require. As my children have gotten older, I have gotten much better at this. I would also add that my

support system of the fathers, grandparents and other family has been huge.
8. With the help of others
9. GOD and praying
10. I maintained the perfect balance by keeping God first.
11. I cannot say that I maintained the perfect balance. I just did what I felt I needed to do.
12. To be honest I'm still working at having a balance. For the most part I'm winging most days.
13. I have never had a balance. I always put my son first, period. I guess now that he is a teenager, I started back dating a few years ago. Now might be some resemblance of balance. I have been dating the same gentleman four years.
14. Well, I was very organized and structured. There was a time for everything I had to do. I made "to-do" lists and pretty much stuck with them.

How did you maintain the perfect balance?

What is your secret to success?

1. Just keep trying. If one thing doesn't work, try something else. My boys are kind, caring men and I am proud that I had a hand in that.
2. Stay strong and focus and look at the light at the end of the tunnel.
3. Prayer, faith and determination
4. I'm optimistic…never one way in or out… Explore your options.
5. Never be afraid to ask for help. Mental, spiritual or financial. Especially when it's for the well-being of my kids.
6. God! There is absolutely no way I would have made it this far by myself.
7. Homing in on my goals, making a plan, allowing some flexibility for changes and not being ashamed to ask for help when I need it. No matter what, nothing deters me from the goals I have laid out for myself and my kids.
8. Staying strong and not giving up.
9. If you have the drive and motivation, go for anything that you want in life 'Cause the sky

is the limit. Get in a field trip that you love and make the best of it.
10. I'm not sure that I feel like I am a success. I am working with what I have.
11. I'm still working on my secret to success.
12. Prayer, faith, never giving up even when obstacles come my way. Obtaining and using the knowledge I've obtained to excel to the next level. Treating people, the way I want to be treated, and showing love, compassion, and kindness.
13. My secret to success is self-worth, having a vision, understanding my personal needs and wants, continuously learning, and building healthy relationships.
14. God...He has placed so many different people in my life along the way that have all somehow been of support to me.
15. My secret is that I am driven, I cried a lot of days and nights, felt alone, felt defeated but I never gave up. I never left my son. My love for

him never diminished, no matter how I felt about his father.

16. My personal determination to show the world that as a single mother, I could be successful in anything that I do with reliance on state assistance. If you put a challenge before me, I strategized how I was going to conquer it. I had friends who were complacent with state assistance, and didn't bother to go to college or trade school to earn a degree, while they were getting help from the state. Later, once that assistance was being cut off...they felt it was too late.

What is your secret to success?

Your Thoughts

How do you respond to people who ask nosy questions, such as (a.) Where is your child's father? (b.) Does the father see your child often? (c.) Does the father pay child support? (d.) Do you get any kind of state assistance? (e.) What name is on your child's birth certificate?

1. The usual answer was "I don't know and don't care."
2. I say, "I'm sorry but I would rather not answer that."
3. (a.) He's around. (b.) He does. (c.) A little nosy, aren't we?!?! (d.) No. (e.) Clarify. I say my situation could happened to any woman. I could have been married and got divorced. Then, hello! I'm a single mother. Especially if it was an ugly divorce. I believe I have had to give that example before.
4. Yes—he is still around and sees him most weekends. No state assistance. My son has his father's last name although the law has now changed in MS.

5. If it's family or a close friend, I will usually address any questions due to the nature of our relationship and knowing they are inquiring for a reason. Anyone else I have no problem saying that's personal or that's none of your business.
6. I tell the truth. I am not ashamed of where I'm at. I don't think we should hide our journey. Some things are private so yes keep it to yourself, but as far as these questions I am honest. I met a single mother who is in the same career as I am, and I asked her questions like this, and she was so open to share her experience. It was nice hearing someone who has been in the same position as myself and they were able to overcome those obstacles. It gave me hope that better is yet to come. Hiding only hinders others.
7. No one has ever actually asked me any of those questions. Those are totally inappropriate questions and I would probably tell them it is none of their business.

8. In my case, I would tell them that's my business. If I wanted them to know I would have told them.

9. If they inquire about where he is at, I'll just say he is around. If he comes around, he comes around. I don't try to force him to take care of them in any kind of way because in the end my children are not missing a meal.

10. People don't ask me those type of questions. My child's father does pay child support but he is not on the birth certificate. Over the years, I have received food stamps and I also have Medicaid.

11. (a) I tell people, "I'm not sure where his dad is." (b) Only two times after our divorce in 2001 and my son is 20 now. (c) No child supports. (d) No state assistance. (e) My child's birth certificate has my name and his dad's name.

12. I really don't get those questions. But if asked, I would answer truthfully. My kids' dad and I are divorced. He was in contact with them but

never really paid any support. He passed away in 2018.

13. I really never experienced this as I have always been a shy, private, and quiet person. So, no one really asked such questions to me.
14. I generally would just answer the questions. Most people in my circle know my situation so it generally doesn't come up. For the most part, I'm honest.
15. It depends. No one of value asks me those questions, but if they did, I would be honest, and educate them.
16. Yes, people would actually ask me these questions. I used to make excuses for the absent father, but as I got older, my response switched to "How can you fix your mouth to ask such nosy questions?" That would usually put them in their place.

How do you respond to people who ask nosy questions, such as (a.) Where is your child's father? (b.) Does the father see your child often? (c.) Does the father pay child support? (d.) Do you get any kind of state assistance? (e.) What name is on your child's birth certificate?

Your Thoughts

Single Mother Syndrome By Choice or By Design 81

As a single mother, do you have any regrets?

1. My biggest regret is not having done more to take care of me during those years. Being alone now is not what I had thought my life would be like.
2. Yes, putting up with some of the things I did for so long and not looking at my value.
3. Plenty, then I think about how my kids are, so I wouldn't change it.
4. No
5. Not really. Not any major ones.
6. Nope!
7. None
8. Having my children so young, but I would not change a thing now.
9. I love my children to death, but if I could change anything, it would be who I had them by. I feel like me and my children didn't deserve the betrayal or [to] have to deal with a man like him. I just wish I knew then what I know now.

10. Sure, I do. One being that I wish I made better choices when it came to who I slept with but we can't change the past.
11. I have no regrets at all. Having my son made me a strong independent woman.
12. No regrets because everything that has taken place made me the person I am today.
13. The only regret that I have as a mother is having to go right back to work shortly after each birth. I didn't have the luxury of staying home with my infant babies because I had to return to work to earn money to take care of us.
14. Yes, with having my oldest so young, I regret not helping her with her schoolwork more. I regret working so much that I couldn't show up to after-school activities she was in. I regret and feel as though I missed out on a lot of her younger years.
15. No, not regarding my son, he is my joy, and my inspiration in life! Sometimes, I wished I

had made a better choice in choosing the individual to bring forth life with.

16. Yes, my biggest regret is that my children did not have an opportunity to form a relationship with their father...by no fault of my own...during their formative years.

As a single mother, do you have any regrets?

When is it the right time for you to date?

1. I started dating a great guy about five years ago. I guess that was the "right" time.
2. When you have learned to love yourself first.
3. My children's father and I were together for 19 years. We have been living apart for about a year. We were hanging on by a thread for several years prior. I am trying to get out on the dating scene. No one will meet my children until I get into a serious dating situation.
4. Unsure...You'll just know.
5. When you feel it's the right time. I don't think there is a specific answer. Everyone is different. I will say it shouldn't be too soon after a big breakup. Everyone (Mom and kids) needs time to heal. Also, people you are dating shouldn't meet the kids until you are ready to date that person exclusively. Especially if there are younger children involved.
6. Oh gosh, I have no idea. I had my daughter at 23 and I'm 31 now. I am now just starting to date. It is a hard balance.

7. That depends on so many factors and everyone's circumstances will require a different answer. I think the mother has to look at what is happening with her kids and herself and if there are any quality options that will make dating worth her time.
8. When you feel you're ready, but not around the kids.
9. I feel like now is the right time…when your children are teenagers. But I will not bring anyone around them until I know that it is serious.
10. When you feel you're ready.
11. After 18.
12. Now that my kids are grown, this is a good time for me to date.
13. I never gave thought as to when to date. The only thing I didn't do was bring a guy to my home to meet my children. For years, my children never met a guy I was dating because most of those relationships ended as short

term, so I didn't see any reason for introductions.

14. I believe when you're ready. When to introduce your children to someone you're dating is a different question. For the most part when you have the time when you can find a balance between yourself, your kids and dating someone.

15. It was the right time when my 10-year-old said, "Mommy I want you to have a friend, and husband to help you so you won't have to do all the work by yourself, Mom you deserve a nice boyfriend."

16. I feel that any time is the right time to date as long as (1) you have a reliable and trustworthy babysitter, and (2) you are able to balance a social life with your parental role.

When is it the right time for you to date?

Your Thoughts

What are some essential qualities for a potential mate?

1. Intelligence, kindness, employed. Someone who will work as hard as I do to be successful.
2. Good with kids, loving, caring, helpful, hardworking.
3. Stable career, well established (house, reliable vehicle), financially secure, having the drive to be a provider, be happy and wanting to grow with one another.
4. Stable, respectful, and seeking God.
5. Stable, God-fearing, good core values, respectful, understands my kids come with me. They are nonnegotiable.
6. They have to like kids. My daughter is the most important person to me and they have to accept and acknowledge that she will always be in the picture. I'd love for them to have a level head and want a family, because that's what we would become eventually.

7. Motivated, love kids, reflective, confident, self-sufficient, shared goals and values and committed to a partnership.
8. Stability, God-fearing, someone who will treat my kids as their own.
9. Someone who has goals, nice personality, sense of humor, their own home, car, job, and someone who likes to have a good time.
10. Honesty, self-aware, commitment, reliable, loyal...to name a few.
11. Kindness, loyalty, income/earnings and attractiveness.
12. Godly man, hard worker, financially stable, lots in common, get along with my children and family.
13. A mate who is a believer of GOD, fun loving, hard worker, a healthy relationship with his family, positive self-esteem, good communicator, trustworthy, learns from mistakes, knows how to reciprocate, enjoys social outings, and chivalrous.

14. Spiritually yoked with me, loving, patience and a parent themselves.
15. Respect - listening to one another, valuing each other's opinions, and listening in a non-judgmental manner.

What are some essential qualities for a potential mate?

What are your thoughts on live-in boyfriends?

1. With older children, probably not a good idea, although a lot of people make it work.
2. Do they treat you well? Do they treat your kids as their own? Are they helpful not living off of you?
3. Not sure
4. It can make or break your child's perception of his mother.
5. You have to really trust the person and make sure that the kids are comfortable with that living arrangement.
6. I'm not sure how I feel about this. At the current moment I don't think I could have one. I'm not saying I won't ever have one, but we would have to [be] moving toward marriage.
7. I believe caution and clarity should be at the forefront of whatever decision is made. How is his presence contributing to the well-being of your household? What will be his role with the children? Who should they listen to if there is dissension? Do you have a similar vision

and set of principles when it comes to child-rearing? How well do you really know and trust this person around your most valuable assets—your children?

8. That was not for me. I did not want a man living in my home.
9. Very skeptical because I have a teenager daughter who I am very protective over as well as my son. But it will have to be someone I have been dealing with for quite some time.
10. As a single mother, a live-in boyfriend is not for me. My daughter is 18 now and will soon be on her own and I'd still be against it. I'm 44 years old so any man I'm dating needs to have his own.
11. When I was younger it was OK to me to have a live-in boyfriend. Now I'm a grown woman that feels you should be married first.
12. Not for me, but I don't judge others.
13. I personally do not believe in living with someone before marriage. Also, I believe if

you move in together the boyfriend may become complacent.

14. I would never allow a man to move in with me. I have two daughters and there's just too much going on. I would never want to put my daughters in that type of situation. I was never put in that type of situation, so I think that may play a lot into how I feel about it.

15. Never, not as long as my son resides with me. I was married before, no children and divorced. No man lives with me unless I'm married to him!

16. Christian, employed (or permanent income), transportation (not public either), love children, love spending time with family, and unselfish.

What are your thoughts on live-in boyfriends?

Describe how overworked or overwhelmed you are from day to day.

1. I was blessed to work close to home and my hours were close to school hours, so although I was tired, I never felt that I was overwhelmed by what I had to do.
2. It's hard being a single mom. It's not easy especially having more than one child.
3. I have little time for myself. My gray hairs are popping up daily. I try and carve out at least [an] hour at night or when I can work out at the gym, I love to do that.
4. Thank God I'm not. When my children were younger and more dependent on me to do things for them it was a little crazy. I would wake up at 6 am, leave my house at 7:30 am and sometimes not return until 8-9 pm. Sometimes later than that. Full-time job, other community responsibilities, cooking, cleaning, practices and games made life very full.

5. I live at home with my dad and brother. I feel like they wait for me to get home to clean. I cannot stand a dirty home. So, when I get back from work and the house is a mess it stresses me out. Other than that, I don't really feel overworked.
6. Well I was raising four children, and working third shift. I slept on Friday and Saturday when my kids were away.
7. I have to get everything done that needs to be done when I get home because after I sit down for maybe 10 minutes, I'm asleep. Some days, it doesn't seem as though I get enough rest.
8. I don't feel overworked. Tired perhaps.
9. I'm self-employed, so it helps that I can set my own hours.
10. I work and I write and produce stage plays and other events. This can be overwhelming yet rewarding.
11. Most days I'm busy from early morning into late nights as I have work during the day and attending to many errands right after work.

This includes checking/responding to emails for myself and my children's schoolteachers. I'm settled for most nights close to 10:30/11:00 pm.

12. This is usually a nonstop day from around 6 am to 8 pm. I'm going to work, coming home after picking them up, then cooking dinner, asking the girls how they've been, seeing if they need help with any homework and finally mommy time.

13. I'm overworked and underpaid, a single head of household with a graduate degree. I am angry that my White female and male counterparts make more salary than I do with the same degree and I have more years of experience! This is the bullshit that burns me up. I want to afford my son the best schools and exposures to travel.

Describe how overworked or overwhelmed you are from day to day.

Your Thoughts

Did you have a co-parenting plan that worked? If yes, what does it look like? If no, are you interested in having a co-parenting plan?

1. No co-parenting. He left our family when the boys were 6 and 8 and didn't see them until our youngest graduated college when he unexpectedly showed up. He did pay some child support, but just enough not to go to jail.
2. No, but yes interested.
3. No, the whole co-parenting thing only works when you have two willing participants. Since my children's father and I split he spends his days working from sunup to sundown, according to him. Over the past two months he has come around more often to help our son with homework. He still has not taken them anywhere in over a year.
4. He sees his dad on weekends mostly.
5. Yes. We split time the best we can with the distance between us. I provide financial support for day-to-day necessities. We split other costs 50/50.

6. I don't really have one. Once upon a time I did but that went out the window. It's hard to have one when the other parent is selfish.
7. With the father of my two oldest children, ages 15 and 17, I attempted a parenting plan and set of agreements, but he was not game at that time. The father of my youngest, who is 7, began with some verbal agreements, but we ended up creating a plan in court. As time has gone on, we have all settled into some assumed positions and understandings. It is far from perfect, but it is better than many. These relationships are muddy and can be hard to navigate. As long as the needs of the children are absolutely center, and all the parents love their children, it will come together.
8. Yes. He keeps the kids on the weekends so I can rest.
9. No, I don't have a plan but will be interested in having one!
10. No, my child's father was absent until my daughter was 14. He had a stroke and almost

died and wanted to right his wrongs. They speak on the phone and have met in person a few times but the relationship is strained.

11. No co-parenting plans.
12. No. My kids are now grown.
13. No. I didn't have any co-parenting plans. At this time, I'm not interested.
14. Yes, my daughter was given her own phone so she can communicate with her father. Fortunately for us, her bus route went past his home, so she could always get off and go to his house whenever she liked and he would drop her off. We rarely communicated at all.
15. Well, my son's dad is an all-around deadbeat, no interaction and no child support prior to court. Support was court ordered only after my son was age 6. I filed when he was 1 year old. So now, the dad is so angry with me he commits to the virtual abandonment of our son!
16. No

Did you have a co-parenting plan that worked? If yes, what does it look like? If no, are you interested in having a co-parenting plan?

Your Thoughts

What strengths do you possess that enhanced your role as a single mother?

1. Well organized, good at time management and financially responsible.
2. Hardworking, staying strong, patience.
3. Recognizing I am only one person carrying multiple loads and responsibilities. Having to be okay with not being able to do everything.
4. Humorous, thinking ahead, preparing, realistic.
5. Always putting the kids first is what I would say is my strength. Sounds normal, but sometimes with co-parenting, other variables can impact your decision-making and you do what works for you, not what's best for your kids. I think for the most part I've been able to keep my personal feelings and my motherhood separate and focus on the big picture.
6. Hard work and determination. I grew up with a family that does not give up or give in.
7. I have always had a love for kids and work with children in my career, so I came with a lot

of knowledge. I am also pretty creative, so I use that to think through a lot of sticky situations. I am a natural planner and I think strong organizational skills can help you keep your life in order.

8. Try to not let the children see me stress or even see me cry sometimes. I get up every morning when it's mornings that I don't want to get up and go to work but I know I have to provide for them 'cause if I don't, who will?

9. It's always been hard for me to identify my strengths as a single mother as I feel I am simply doing what a mother who loves her child does. Over the years I have been ambitious on working towards goals and dreams but things have not panned out for me.

10. Time management, communication, people management, problem solving and organizational skills.

11. Faith in God, great example in my parents and the will to survive.

12. I have a healthy support system, a healthy self-esteem, and I pamper myself.
13. I have faith, I have the love and support of my dad and financially at times, and I have a sense of fortitude and determination that would not allow me to ever quit!

What strengths do you possess that enhanced your role as a single mother?

Your Thoughts

Were you logistically (i.e., had living space for your child, could take a leave of absence from work, had childcare arrangements, etc.) prepared to become a single mother?

1. I did have a home that I kept when my husband left. He moved out of state.
2. Not at all!
3. When I first had my daughter, I was employed at Home Depot. I made a decent paycheck for someone in their 20s. I have insurance. But thinking long term, no I was not ready. I wasn't ready when I had my son and I was 30 and my employment situation was much better.
4. Yes!
5. No, I was not.
6. I was not. I just knew it would work out. It just had to. I wasn't going to give up on being able to provide a good life for my child.
7. When I got pregnant with my eldest child, I was absolutely unprepared financially and logistically. When I learned I was pregnant, I

ended up moving in with my mother who was living in another state at the time. While staying with my mama, I began planning our future. I had not graduated from high school, so I took my GED test at 26 and passed. I then applied to a community college and began school two months after the birth of my daughter. Seventeen years later, I am prepping to complete my Ph.D. and my daughter is graduating from high school!

8. No.
9. No, I was not. Everything was new to me. I had to figure out where we were going to stay which we moved with my mother for about a month until I found a place and had to commute back and forth. Their aunt would still keep them for me if I needed her to!
10. Yes, I had all the things I needed as well as the support required to be a single mother and what I didn't have I made sure I got it.
11. Yes.

12. I was able to take leave, but I wasn't prepared to be a single mom.//
13. I was 23 years old when I had my first child still living at home. My grandmother watched my firstborn until he was able to go to Head Start. By the time I had my last second child, I had to primarily rely on daycare centers.
14. I most likely might have been better off. I was educated, owned a home, had a profession, but it was hard to get FMLA just 16 years ago! Employers were biased against single mothers! Imagine that! I couldn't take higher paying positions because I couldn't travel for work as no family members would keep my son if I traveled out of town and overnight.

Were you logistically (i.e., had living space for your child, could take a leave of absence from work, had childcare arrangements, etc.) prepared to become a single mother?

Your Thoughts

How did you handle the stress and pressure of single parenting?

1. My faith kept me going.
2. It was hard but I just looked at the positive things in life.
3. I cried and prayed about it.
4. Venting when needed.
5. I never really felt any pressure. Their dad has always been present and we've always had a strong village of support. I think the pressures I have felt are normal pressures that come with being a parent.
6. When I found out I was pregnant I took some serious time out to decide if I could raise a child by myself. I had no idea how I was going to do it but I told myself I would take things one day at a time and trust God.
7. I learned to put pride aside and ask for help when I need it.
8. I went in the bathroom and cried and came out feeling OK. My kids never knew how stressed I was until they got in their teens.

9. Talked to my friend who is also a single parent. I did a lot of praying and was determined I wasn't going to let that get the best of me.
10. Life is stressful, so I really can't say that being a single mother made it any more stressful. I simply did what I had to do to survive and take care of myself and my daughter.
11. I prayed all day and night.
12. Prayer, faith in God, talking to family.
13. I relied on my favorite activities which involved spending time at the lake or beach as well as taking long drives in my car which I continue such outings currently.
14. Honestly, I just did it, sick or well, hurt, crying or happy...It had to be done and my love for my son was tremendously fierce!

How did you handle the stress and pressure of single parenting?

Your Thoughts

What calms you?
1. Prayer, music, and time outside.
2. Coloring, and cuddling my children.
3. Talking to someone I trust.
4. Musical stimulation articles.
5. Writing, meditation, and going to the movies alone.
6. Cleaning. I love cleaning!
7. I meditate, go to the gym, listen to jazz and soft classical music.
8. Meditation
9. Music, playing my games on my phone or even having a little ladies' night and just venting.
10. Alone time and smoking weed.
11. Exercising.
12. Prayer, talking to my family, hot bath, and soothing music.
13. I love going to the lake/beach. Such outing is calming to me. I love walking barefoot in the sand and on the grass. I love sitting on the pier watching and listening to the waves of the

water crashing. I love taking long drives especially at night on summer nights to feel a nice breeze and look at the night lights all of which is calming to me.

14. Now, my faith, my inner peace, I don't allow anyone or anything to disturb my peace, or detract from my joys in life

15. Peace and quiet while sipping on a cup of coffee. Eating chocolates. Reading a Danielle Steel book. Watching a movie.

What calms you?

Your Thoughts

What is your occupation?

1. Office manager
2. I'm a care worker.
3. Supervisor in foster care
4. Teacher
5. Entrepreneur
6. Pilot for Endeavor Air (Delta Connection)
7. Ph.D. candidate in education policy
8. Retired manager at Target
9. Customer service representative at a bank
10. I was a receptionist and activity aide at Willowbrook Manor for four years but just recently got offered a job at Davita Dialysis to be a phlebotomist, which I am really excited about.
11. Dish tank operator
12. Self-employed
13. State of Michigan employee—property analyst with the MI Dept. of Transportation
14. Psyche therapist
15. I am a clinically licensed medical social worker for a major hospital in northeast Ohio.

16. Retired

What is your occupation?

Your Thoughts

What was the most difficult part of being a single mother?

1. Not always having the funds to do the things the boys wanted to do.
2. Trying to do everything on your own.
3. Not being where I wanted to be in life before having a child(ren).
4. Homework and school transportation.
5. Not seeing my kids every day.
6. I don't like that she doesn't really have a strong father figure in her life. I kind of get a break while I'm at work but I'm still making sure everything is being taken care of.
7. I had a hard time initially understanding that everyone may not do as you believe they should do regarding stepping in and up for your children. Regardless, as their mother, I have to handle business and make things happen. I don't have the luxury of excuses for not providing whatever my kids need materially, emotionally and mentally.
8. Leaving my kids when I had to work.

9. Not raising my children in a two-parent home like I planned to do when I had children.
10. Raising a teenage son who was seeking attention from his father.
11. Not being able to have a break from parenting. Raising my son alone. My family lived in another state, but was there when I needed them. It takes a village to raise a child.
12. Finances. Being the only one bringing in income was very challenging most times.
13. The most difficult part in being a single mother was not having a two-parent home when they were small. I never wanted to be a single mother. I had always seen myself as a mother with a husband. I believe in a two-parent home to bring a nice balance to the child/children.
14. Dealing with disciplinary situations. Finding time to help and support your children when their schoolwork is difficult and of course the financial aspect.
15. The loneliness. The scary time when I lost my job for three months until I got a new one and

didn't know if I could feed my baby! I was scared. His father I remember would give me $5.00 to buy 2 gallons of milk...sad times.

16. Having my children ask where was their father because he was too busy to come visit with them. Not being able to give my children the things they wanted.

What was the most difficult part of being a single mother?

What is your favorite part about being a single mother?

1. I don't have to answer for how I spend my money. My decisions are not questioned or reversed.
2. You get to know you did it on your own and your kids will be proud one day.
3. Seeing my kids evolve.
4. My body produced a healthy and strong kid effortlessly!!! That I take very good care of.
5. I just love being a mom.
6. I get her all to myself—hahaha.
7. I just love my babies! They are my happy place. They are funny, sweet and smart and I can't wait to see what they will become.
8. When my children would come up to me and give me a hug and say they love me
9. Throughout it all it made me to be a strong woman and my children seeing that I am not letting no weapon formed against me prosper.
10. Knowing that I have raised a smart, talented, and great human being.

11. Having an obedient son.
12. The relationship I was able to develop with my children. Being able to be an example to them to help them live a good life.
13. I really didn't enjoy being a single mother for the beliefs. Although I will share that my favorite part of being a mother has been watching the growth in each of my children. It's a wonderful experience to see each one develops their own personality.
14. To me there is no favorite part of being a single mother. All the favorite parts for me just come in from basically and simply being a mother. I would have preferred not to be a single mother.
15. My favorite part of being a single mom is the joy and pride in seeing my beautiful, intelligent, and handsome son do all of what I raised him to be and do. He is such a funny guy and fun to be around!
16. My children's hugs and love.

What is your favorite part about being a single mother?

Do you attend single-parent support groups where you live? If yes, how effective are they? If not, would you be interested in receiving information about single-parent support groups?

1. No, although I did attend Adult Children of Alcoholics meetings and those helped with the parenting and the adult issues I was dealing with.
2. No, and yes interested.
3. No. If there was one in my area.
4. No.
5. No and no thank you.
6. I did not. I have a pretty good support system right now. A couple mothers who are pilots and some who are not. We all help each other out.
7. No.
8. No, I don't but will be willing to receive information that you have.
9. No. I did attend a stay-at-home mom group when my daughter was an infant and I wasn't working but I didn't feel a real connection with

the women as they were all White and if I can recall correctly most if not all were married.

10. No.
11. No, I did not. My children are now grown, not interested in support groups.
12. No, I have never attended single-parent groups, although I believe such groups can be very helpful with providing emotional support, learning how to do self-care, and learning new and helpful ways on parenting.
13. No, I have never attended a parenting group of any kind. No, I would not like to receive any information about parenting groups. If I were younger or thought of having more children maybe that would be something I would consider.
14. I attended one single-parent group, once. It was creepy because the single dads hit on me…yuck!
15. There is a Black Single Mother Support Group that I participate in on Facebook. If there were an in-person group, I would attend.

Do you attend single-parent support groups where you live? If yes, how effective are they? If not, would you be interested in receiving information about single-parent support groups?

Additional comments and/or suggestions
1. A mother should plant seeds that grow and sustain their child in life and flourish idealistic approaches that adhere to freedom! That's what living is about!
2. Single mothers rock!!
3. I appreciate your efforts to highlight single mothers so that we all receive the reverence we so richly deserve.
4. I pray for much success for your upcoming books and all of your endeavors!
5. Being a single parent is truly both hard work and rewarding.
6. To stay strong, have patience, and don't let your children rule you. It might be cute while they are babies, but when they turn 4 or 5 it's time to put a stop to it.

Additional comments and/or suggestions

Your Thoughts

CHAPTER FOUR

Message from The Author

Now that you have finished reading the book, what do you think? Did you fill in your thoughts following each question? We are inviting you to attend a *free* **Meet the Author and Contributors Virtual Zoom Event on May 7, 2022, at 6:30 pm** EST. Use the space below to write questions or comment you may have for us. Register free at: http://evite.me/epTVHScR9Z Or, email the author at drbrendabrown9836@gmail.com

_____
_____
_____
_____
_____

APPENDIX A

Single Mothers Ministry in the Church

By: Sean Teis, LifeFactors.org

Pray and ask God to help you make a plan to consistently minister to the single moms in your circles of influence. In everything you do, point them to God! This is not about us; it is about them experiencing god as their Heavenly Father!

WHEN GOD BRINGS THESE INDIVIDUALS AND/OR FAMILIES INTO OUR LIVES AND MINISTRY'S WE ARE RESPONSIBLE TO HELP THEM!

Before reading the list below think of things a good husband does for his wife. He surprises his wife with coffee, a note, a gift, etc. He helps take care of their home, their children, their life, etc. Now picture him being gone. Single moms are facing this reality every day!

We encourage you to try to get your whole church to reach out and help meet these families' needs and show them that God is the one who is filling their voids. It is not just about one person ministering to them but about many. Our whole goal is to point them to Christ, and let them know that He will be there and that He is their hero!

NOTE OF ENCOURAGEMENT

Write them a note with the message of: "You can do this, we are here for you, we believe in you, and through God, you can succeed this year!" Ask them if they will share their goals for the year. Ask them about prayer requests for the year. Devote this year to consistently pray for them. Ask them later about updates for their prayer requests. Devise plans to meet those needs through the people and resources of your church.

LAUNCH A SINGLE MOM GROUP

The beginning of the year is a great time to launch a single mom ministry in your church. If you can lead the single mom to a personal relationship with Jesus and disciple her then her children will have a better home and they may have a higher chance of being reached and discipled themselves as well. Consider launching a single mom group that meets weekly or monthly. Consider hosting the single mom group at times when your church already has childcare such as a Sunday school hour, a Sunday night, or a Wednesday night. If your group is held monthly, they could rotate into other ministries as well the other three weeks of the month. This might help them get even more connected to the church. Or make it a special night each month to just focus on these families and not take them away from regularly scheduled programming. At the end of completing the 30 days of the Single Mom Journey consider having a graduation ceremony/party for them! Consider also having activities monthly or quarterly to just spend some time with them and their children. You can find activity ideas through reading through The Single Mom Year Monthly Ideas that we share! However, you decide to do this, it would be a great resource and help for the single moms in your church and community!

WARM THEM UP WITH SOME COFFEE OR TEA

Let them know your church loves them through a random coffee or a gift card to their favorite coffee shop! Or, stop by their house or workplace with their favorite latte, tea, Frappuccino, etc.!

WINTER HELP!

Go to where they are and help them! Do they need any work done on their home or on their car to get them through the winter and to possibly lower their heating costs in their home or to keep them safe as they travel? Are their car tires good enough to last them through the winter? Do they need help shoveling snow off their driveway, sidewalk, or off the roof of their home? Do they need help getting any tree limbs off the roof of their home? For the non-snow areas, this might be the best time to do some outside work on their homes. Take a crew from the church and get done what you are able to! Try to get their children or teens involved in these projects too if they are capable! Monthly or quarterly visiting their homes one Saturday a month and helping with them would mean the world to these families! These are mission trips available in our own backyards! The workers for these days will also most likely be blessed for their work as well! It is a win-win situation for everyone involved!

MENTORING

The beginning of the year is a great time to launch a mentoring ministry for single moms' children. This can be a formal program or just finding caring adults with strong Christian testimonies to spend quality time with the fatherless children of your church and community. As is the same with your children's ministry make sure that it is safe for the child and volunteer and work to never allow volunteers and children to be one-on-one. If you are an individual Christian that wants to become a mentor then start helping a fatherless family in your circle of influence such as a co-worker, a niece or nephew, etc.! Many single moms crave finding a godly man or woman or a godly couple to help them guide their child or teen. Spending time with these children and teens in a safe environment weekly, bi-monthly, or monthly usually is a major key in helping them overcome the statistics!

GIVE THEM SOME R&R

Going sled riding, ice-skating, or another winter type of event or activity? Then consider inviting the single moms' children to go along with you! Single moms often need and want some help which includes having some time to step away for a bit. Just watching the kids for a few hours would be a blessing to them. Plus, during this, you might also get to spend some quality mentoring time with their children and teens. Also, if the guardian gets some R&R, they should be able to better handle their children in stressful times!

BE A PRAYER PARTNER

Become a prayer partner with a single mom, her children, or their entire family. Make sure to partner a lady with the single mom or the girls. Fatherless individuals, single moms, and almost everyone love it when someone asks if we have any prayer requests, and then they follow up later about that prayer request. This is an encouragement to most. Do this for fatherless families. Keep a prayer list. Ask them how you can pray. Follow up with them about the requests. If it is a need look at ways that you or someone you know can help answer that request. Keep asking them on a regular basis (monthly, quarterly, etc.) about new prayer requests and follow-up about previous requests that they had. Also, make sure to really be praying for those requests for them. What a connection that this makes between their family and your church. We all want to be known, we all want to be loved, we all want to been encouraged, and this does all three!

GET THEM A DEVOTIONAL TO DO:

Provide some resources for them to grow in their walk with God. Get them a Biblically/Doctrinally sound general devotional or to view [Life Factors Store](#).

ONCE A MONTH PROVIDE A MEAL

Once a month have a church member bring supper to their home. This will give the single mom the night off from cooking. If she works, she will REALLY appreciate this! Rotate church members if possible so that the single mom can meet and build friendships with others.

ONCE A MONTH OR QUARTERLY PROVIDE GROCERIES

Buy groceries - ask them what they like or don't like - it can be overwhelming to get things that they don't like, but feel bad because it was gifted to them. Do this in raw form - possibly consider something such as Hello Fresh, Blue Apron, etc. (Just ideas, no sponsorship here =) Or ask them to message you their grocery list for the week, or some items that they need, and do a pick up at a local grocery store for them. Or go in a toiletry item's direction and provide for some or all of their needs.

GIVE THEM A NIGHT OFF

Single moms often need and want some help which includes having some time to step away for a bit. Just watching the kids for a few hours, would be a blessing to them. You could do this monthly, quarterly or as often as possible. Plus, you will get to spend some time with the kids. Also, if the guardian gets some headspace, they should be able to better handle their children in stressful times!

HELP MENTOR THEIR CHILDREN

Many single moms crave finding a godly man or woman or a godly couple to help them guide their child or teen. Spending time with these children and teens in a safe environment weekly, bi-monthly, or monthly usually is a major key in helping them overcome the statistics! We also have digital resources to help churches better disciple fatherless families and we are looking for at least one church in every county of the United States to partner with.

KEEP TRACK OF SPECIAL DATES

Inquire from these families about special dates such as birthdays, significant death dates, and any other special dates. Keep these dates on a calendar with

notifications. Celebrate with them or encourage them on these days through a text, call, email, message, card, gift, meal, etc.

APPENDIX B

Family Fusion: Single Parent, Value Yourself

"Being a single parent is twice the work, twice the stress and twice the tears but also twice the hugs, twice the love and twice the pride." – Unknown

By: Reverend Haynesley Griffith

Single parenting has to be very tough, especially if that parent's support system is weak or non-existent. Single parenting can result from situations like unplanned or planned pregnancy, divorce, death of a parent or spouse, rape, desertion, adoption and even in some instances, when two parents live together but only one takes on the parenting responsibilities.

The issue continues to be a perennial social worry worldwide. I have heard several expressions from single parents: "This child is driving me crazy"; "I can't deal with this child"; "I just feel like giving up"; "I feel like a failure"; "I don't know what else to do with this child"; "This child has a demon"; "I feel like taking something and knocking off the head of this child". I have also met single parents who said the very opposite to the forgoing remarks of frustration, and spoke of how much they cherished their children and see them as extremely special, despite annoying negative behaviours.

Although God's ideal from the beginning has been for children to grow up with male and female parents within the context of marriage, as stated in Genesis 2:21-25, single parents should never be viewed as second class citizens. In fact, some single parents, mothers or fathers have been able, with the grace of God and excellent support structures, to raise outstanding men and women of whom the world is justly proud.

In this series on single parenting, I shall take a look at some of the main concerns with which many single parents may be faced and offer some suggestions that can assist in working through those issues.

The realities of single parenting cannot be ignored. In the United States, one of every three homes are managed by a single parent; in the United Kingdom, that number is one in every four, and in the Caribbean an average of about 45 percent of homes are cared for by single parents. The percentage of women compared to men attending to their children within a single home environment continues to be far higher. However, research is now showing that there is an increase of men taking on single parent responsibility.

For those who have experienced single parenting as teens and young adults, the harsh realities cannot be explained in words. Teenage and young adult single parents may suffer a delay or even unfulfillment of some important dreams and goals. Furthermore, coming up against some very difficult obstacles, including the social and economic barriers for which they were not previously prepared, often proved overwhelming. Since the teens are also struggling with their own adolescent adjustments, creating an environment of warmth and love for the baby's myriad of needs becomes an uphill task.

More mature single parents may experience some of the same struggles as the teenager, but ongoing loneliness and trying to balance home, work and self-improvement studies frequently create stress.

One crucial area with which some single parents struggle is valuing themselves. The more value and worth you place on yourself in all areas of your life, the more benefits your children may reap as they mature. Self-value has many facets; single parents should consider the following:

• **Value yourself emotionally.**

Whatever may have caused you to be a single parent, never see yourself as a mistake or less than a person because of your condition. There are times when those feelings may come to your mind to make you think of yourself as less than valuable. Although you cannot stop those thoughts from coming, try not to accept them. Feelings of guilt at times may make it difficult for you to go forward with your life. Try not to get into the habit of blaming yourself and trying to compensate by spoiling your child.

Years ago, a distraught single mum told me she felt less than valuable because guilt feelings were making it difficult for her to advance. She was encouraged over time to change the negative concept she had developed of herself. She did. Today, she is an outstanding citizen with a sharply focused child.

- **Value yourself socially.**

The one thing you cannot change is the fact that you are a single parent. Therefore, surround yourself with positive thinking people who will encourage you to see your life as not having come to a full stop, but instead, progressing to a positive and wonderful future. Get out of the house and join a well-organized single parents' support group or even start one yourself. In interacting with others, you may find out that you have similar issues and may learn how to cope with certain challenges. In general, continue to develop your social life within reason, considering the reality that you have a child or children to whom you have serious responsibilities.

- **Value yourself intellectually.**

Because you are a single parent, it does not mean that you have lost your ability to use your brain to create great things. I know of single parents who were left alone with the burden of struggling through life with their children. Some of them, with the help of counsellors, painstakingly revised their future goals and devised means and ways of realizing those goals. Today they look back with a great sense of accomplishment for themselves as well as their children. Never surrender yourself to be at the mercy of others to be owned by them. Cherish and develop your intellect.

- **Value yourself spiritually.**

In God's sight you are of great value. Others may think otherwise. Ignore them. Place your trust in the all-wise, all-knowing, all-understanding God whose love for you is unconditional. Many single parents have told me how He helped them when the going got really tough. It is in Him that you "live and move and exist" (Acts 17:28).

When you value yourself as a single parent, the chances of placing a high premium on your children are very great. You cannot take your precious children further than you yourself have gone.

APPENDIX C

The Saga of Single Parenting

By Reverend Tony Evans

The story of Hagar has some real-life lessons for single parents. We first meet Hagar in Genesis 16, where she was the servant of Sarai, who along with her husband Abram (this was just before their names were changed) were unable to have children.

In the custom of their day, barren women in Sarai's situation would bring in another woman who would bear the husband's child and thus act as a surrogate. Hagar became a surrogate for Sarai.

When Hagar got pregnant Sarai became jealous and drove Hagar out of the house. Pregnant and alone, with no Abram or any other male to support and protect her, she found herself wandering in the wilderness. Hagar was about to become a single parent because she got caught in someone else's plan.

But then the Angel of the Lord (Jesus pre-incarnate) went out to the wilderness for the benefit of this single mother-to-be. In other words, Jesus showed up. That was good news for Hagar.

If you are a single parent, that's also good news for you. When you have been rejected, when the father or mother of your child is nowhere to be found, God knows the situation you are in and He knows where to find you. He loves and shows great compassion on you. When you hurt, He feels it. He knows your loneliness, stigma, and pain. After all, He experienced the fullness of all three on the cross.

When God showed up, He told Hagar to name her son Ishmael, which meant "God hears and God knows." Every time she would use that name, she would remember something about God. That's the beauty of the grace of God for a single parent. Hagar is out on her own with no help, but God says, "I know."

In verse 13 Hagar responded. Giving God the name El Roi, she declared, "Thou art a God who sees."

Do you know that God sees you? The circumstances you are in? Out there in the desert all alone with no one to provide for, give you spiritual and emotional covering, and protection. He is not unaware of what you are going through. No matter what you are going through, God says, "I see. I hear. I know."

The saga of Hagar does not end here. In Genesis 21 we see that Hagar, instructed by the Lord, has gone back to Sarah. By now Sarah has had Isaac, the son God had promised her and Abraham (their names had been changed by then also).

One day when Sarah saw Ishmael making fun of Isaac (v. 9) she said, "Not in my house you won't!" She had Abraham put them out. Hagar, along with her son, were homeless again and left to wander in the wilderness alone. Now, she was a bona fide single mother.

This is a classic single-parent scenario—one that, with a few changes of detail and geography, could easily be repeated today. Hagar lost her home, she had a teenage son to take care of, and she was on the streets, so to speak, with no money in her pockets. She was thirsty and probably hungry. She feared that her boy would die. In despair she sat down and cried.

When the Son of God showed up again, He asked Hagar, "What is the matter with you?" (v. 17). He was saying, "Hagar, have you forgotten what I did for you earlier? How I found you out in the wilderness when you were pregnant and Sarah had chased you away? Do you think I am going to remember you one minute and forget you the next? You yourself said I am the God who sees. Do you think that now I have gone blind?"

Single parent, God has not gone blind. He sees, He hears, and He knows. You may be in a far from ideal situation, but you have an ideal God.

The greatest thing you can do is have a passion for God, because single mother, when you have a passion for God you have Someone who will be a Father to your child and a Husband and protector to you. Single father, when you know God you have

Someone to lean on who understands a father's heart and desires for his children.

As He was with Hagar, so is He with you…the God who sees and knows and cares.

APPENDIX D

Single Parenting: Questions Your Child May Ask and How to Answer Them

By: Chris Russo, Babygaga.com

There are many difficult jobs in this world that I will be the first to give a tip of the hat to: men and women who serve their country, here and abroad; health care professionals who save lives every day; teachers who help shape the minds of tomorrow and finally single parents.

Now before anyone gets in a huff asking, "well what about regular parents?" Let me tell you that I feel your pain, and I know the trials and tribulations that you and your partner go through on a day to day basis.

It isn't easy, both my partner and I agree, but I think that in itself says it all; if two people find it hard, what about one?

While I admire and respect single parents the world over, I certainly don't envy them. Don't get me wrong, I love being a parent, and from it has sprung some of my fondest and most eternal memories, but looking back, I am quite confident that I would have had a nervous breakdown if I had to go it alone, and that's just from a logistical standpoint (meaning keeping them alive), forget about the actual having to 'parent' them and answering their questions as their little minds grow more and more curious.

All children grow more inquisitive with age, and this can lead to some pretty difficult questions to answer for parents, but perhaps none can be as sensitive as those asked of a single parent by their child; for their situation is unique and in being so come with some rather unique questions.

Though not a product of a single-parent home; my partner is, as well as a number of friends and acquaintances, and it was through this inquiry that I could put together some of the most common questions asked by children to single parents as well as some helpful advice for answering the tough ones that are bound to come up.

Where Did My Mom/Dad Go? (or any variation of why they only have one parent). For the record, I cringed while writing that question for I imagine it to be one of the most difficult questions to answer, not only because of how personal and emotional the answer it might be, but also, (and I think this will be an ongoing theme here) because you have to take into account who is asking the question. Before you answer this question, it is important for you as a single parent to assess the situation and asked yourself a few questions:

- What exactly did happen to your partner? (if there was one)
- Is it appropriate for children? - Now I have always been a big proponent of telling children the truth, but some

things were not meant for children's ears.

- How old are they? - There is a fine line between age and maturity, and it is up to you to decide which trumps which when speaking to your child about difficult subject matter.

After honestly answering these questions, you should have a better idea as to your child's ability to process information, and to what degree that is, will largely determine when they are ready to hear the answer, regardless of when they ask. In the meantime, my suggestion would be to tell them that every family is different but no less important; some have a mom and dad, some two dads or two moms, and others just one. And just to cover my bases, in the rare instance that there is no reason not to tell your child at any age why they only have one parent, then I would always encourage you to do so and tell children the truth.

How Come _____ Has A Mom and A Dad? - If I was a betting man, and you were a single parent, what do you think the odds are that this question had been asked of you, maybe after school one day or when your child goes over to a friend's house for the first time? I am going to guess pretty good. Do you remember what it was like to be a child? No? Me either, but I do have two of them, and unless things are exactly even and equal between the two of them, nobody is happy in my house. This seems to be a universal among the age impaired, and that is an unwavering feeling of equality; one in which for a child, it can be taken as a personal affront if one of their contemporaries has more of something, parents included. Perhaps that is why this question is so commonly fielded by single parents, but it doesn't have to be a difficult one to answer, all you have to do is tell the truth, and a universal truth at that. I am a firm believer in that everything happens for a reason; some have more because they need more, others less for the same reason. I also believe that no child should live or be brought up under a deficit or thinking about their situation as one. So, when fielded with this question, try this:

"_____ has two parents because he needs two parents, and you have one because you only need one. Just like an octopus has 8 arms, and a fish has none; it doesn't make one better than other; they just need different things to be who they are." (Please feel free to paraphrase).

Do They Still Love Me? - Kids really do say the darnedest things, and when it comes to the questions, they ask, I think it often has more to do with being smart than being funny. Children it seems are growing up faster and faster these days and a lot has to do with the seemingly endless amount of information available to them at their fingertips. That being said, children are probably more aware, then we would like to think when it comes to making babies, but for today we will simply leave it at 'it involves two people,', and we can say they know this with certainty if they are asking you the aforementioned question. The answer: YES. It's always yes, come on people! We are talking about children, cute (mostly) adorable (hopefully), but most of all lovable children, and if there is one thing, a child can absolutely not get enough of is love. I don't care what happened to their other parent (in the kindest way possible), because wherever they are, if they talk to them, or they don't, if they are alive or dead, it doesn't matter; the answer is always the same. Children need to know their parents love them, maybe even more when only one of them is around.

What Happened to Mom/Dad? - You might be thinking that this question seems oddly similar to 'Where did Mom/Dad go?' and you would be right, but I want you to think about it in a different way; mainly your child being a bit older asking the question. While your children are young, it is wise and makes sense to shield them from unnecessary pain and heartache, but as they grow older, and inevitably smarter (think Santa Clause) sooner, or later, they deserve to know what happened. This might be difficult depending on the specifics of your situation, but take this as an opportunity to teach your child an important lesson about life, and that is that sometimes the answers to questions aren't necessarily ones we like to hear. In the long run, however, you will be doing your child a favor as shielding them only serves them for so long.

Are You Going to Go Away Too? -No, no, no, NO! Well, maybe one would suffice. Children need to feel they are supported, that they aren't alone, and that they are loved, and you being their parent kind of puts you at the top of that list to fulfill. While it is impossible to predict the future and what life might throw your way, children need to know that you will never leave them. And I say firmly, regardless of what happens, that a part of you will always be with your child and them with you.

Will I Get A New One? I think it is with most certainty that this question has been posed in some form or other to every single parent who has ever dated, and it makes sense. Children for lack of a better word are 'new'; they're wide-eyed, expectant, and unfamiliar with the complexity of adult relationships.

Combine that with seeing their friends having both parents and you with boyfriend or girlfriend might make them wonder. It's only natural for children to want to fill what they perceive as a missing part of their lives, and this can very easily be transferred to a parental figure.

In my opinion, I think it is wise to discuss the possibility of new relationships blossoming into something more serious with your children, because it is such a reality in today's world, and there is nothing wrong with that.

Sometimes love takes a few tries, and sometimes love can happen a few times, but I think it's important to reinforce to your child that nobody who joins your family is there to replace anyone, but rather to add their own personal touch to the already great thing you have going.

Can I Come? While this question is a pretty common one to be had by children, I think it is one that comes up more often, or perhaps that is felt more deeply when it relates to a single-parent family. It isn't hard to imagine that a child with only one parent will form a much stronger bond with them than children of a more traditional family dynamic. That is because it is all, they have ever known, so it is easy for them to become attached and even rather protective of their sole parent. As wonderful as it can be to have your child want to come with you wherever you go (for as we all know it doesn't last) it is important to establish boundaries with your child, so that you can still live a life outside of your child, as well as help ward off the ever growing co-dependency problem that seems to be affecting more and more families.

APPENDIX E

FAQ's & Resources

HealthyChildren.org (2015, November 21), *The Perfect Family*. https://healthychildren.org/English/family-life/family-dynamics/Pages/The-Perfect-Family.aspx

HealthyChildren.org (2015, November 21), *Stresses of Single Parenting*. https://www.healthychildren.org/English/family-life/family-dynamics/types-of-families/Pages/Stresses-of-Single-Parenting.aspx

Single Mothers by Choice. (n.d.). *Frequently asked questions*. https://www.singlemothersbychoice.org/about/faq/

Hasche, J. (n.d.). *FAQ*. https://www.singlemothersurvivalguide.com/frequentlyaskedquestions/

Pennock, S. (n.d.) *Scholarships and grants for single mothers - frequently asked questions*.

https://ezinearticles.com/?Scholarships-And-Grants-For-Single-Mothers---Frequently-Asked-Questions&id=5165564

A single parent support group—Parents Without Partners. https://www.parentswithoutpartners.org/HTML/contact.html

Family and personal growth courses from Wildwood Church. https://real-life.wildwoodchurch.com/felt-needs/single-parent/?gclid=Cj0KCQiAzMGNBhCyARIsANpUkzPUQ7yuS7H-7SowIL95haQ3AnAAI3Bh62mjyoL7cUmaU90WZNcYVSYaAuDLEALw_wcB

Smith, J. (n.d.). *10 of the best books all single moms should read* https://www.graceforsingleparents.com/books-for-single-moms/

Proud Happy Mama. (n.d.). *50+ powerful single mom quotes for single mothers.* https://proudhappymama.com/single-mom-quotes/

Miles, T. (2018). *Love Life Again: Finding Joy When Life Is Hard.*

TerKeurst, L. (2018). *It's Not Supposed to Be This Way: Finding Unexpected Strength When Disappointments Leave You Shattered*

Maggio, J. (2017). *Overwhelmed: The Life of a Single Mom* (2nd ed.).

Cloud, H., & Townsend, J. (2001). *Boundaries with Kids: How Healthy Choices Grow Healthy Children.*

Furtick, S. (2015). *Crash the Chatterbox: Hearing God's Voice Above All Others.*

Whitehurst, T. (2010). *God Loves Single Moms: Practical Help for Finding Confidence, Strength, and Hope.*

Gatehouse Sober Community. (2019, July 12). *How to deal with a lack of family support.* https://www.gatehousesobercommunity.com/how-to-deal-with-a-lack-of-family-support/

Newbreak Church. (n.d.). *The small shift that can make a big difference for your kids.* https://newbreak.church/small-shift-big-difference/?gclid=Cj0KCQiAzMGNBhCyARIsANpUkzPYHcCDKYkTYuEv6qdmQ2lEPHOitPBiOfxj-jeQxqt_fTcQ4Ybn6y8aAhgdEALw_wcB

Lindholm, M. (2016, November 23). *8 mental health challenges single moms face.* https://www.talkspace.com/blog/8-mental-health-challenges-single-moms-face/

Smith, S. (2020, August 6). *15 true facts about single parenting you may not know.* https://www.marriage.com/advice/parenting/6-true-facts-about-single-parenting/

Dallas, A. (2021, July 26). *The disadvantages of single-parent homes.*

https://www.bgcmsdelta.org/the_disadvantages_of_si ngle_parent_homes?gclid=Cj0KCQiAzMGNBhCyA RIsANpUkzNHldU-9mpsZLJKVrmlYSFkjbeW5e0YS8xjdQsMWIY231 ZVowO0uOMaAnSvEALw_wcB

Kear, N. C. (n.d.). *An emotional survival guide for single moms: 7 solutions from mothers who have walked miles in your shoes.* http://www.seleni.org/advice-support/2018/3/13/an-emotional-survival-guide-for-single-moms

Porter, R. (2021, September 23). *Is dating single moms too complicated?* https://www.regain.us/advice/dating/is-dating-single-moms-too-complicated/

Daily devotionals for single mothers by Rev. Delman Coates. https://delmancoates.org/daily-devotionals?gclid=Cj0KCQiAzMGNBhCyARIsANp UkzMFDC2eBwo_aSwM_MLv5hbwd_91SuL2vLc Km8qXL0HeVpV2GwgrKfAaAoKaEALw_wcB

Samuels, K. (2020, February 1). *5 myths & 5 facts about single mothers.* https://www.babygaga.com/myths-facts-single-mothers/

Mayo Clinic. (2020, April 10). *Single parent? Tips for raising a child alone* https://www.mayoclinic.org/healthy-lifestyle/childrens-health/in-depth/single-parent/art-20046774

APPENDIX F

Bibliography

Evans, Tony Rev. The Urban Alternative *The Saga of Single Parenting*. Retrieved from https://tonyevans.org/blog/the-saga-of-single-parenting

Griffith, H. Rev. (2015, March 4). Family Fusion: Single parent, value yourself. Retrieved from https://www.nationnews.com/2015/03/04/family-fusion-single-parent-value-yourself-1/

HealthyChildren.org (2015, November 11), *Caring For Your School Aged Child*. Retrieved from https://healthychildren.org/English/family-life/family-dynamics/Pages/The-Perfect-Family.aspx

Robinson, M. J. (2014, January 17). The single mother syndrome. *Far from Flawless*. Retrieved from http://farfromflawlesslife.blogspot.com/2014/01/the-single-mother-syndrome.html

Russo, Chris (2016, FEB 24). *Single Parenting: Questions Your Child May Ask and How to Answer Them.* Retrieved from https://www.babygaga.com/single-parenting-questions-your-child-may-ask-and-how-to-answer-them/

Teis, Sean (2022, January 28) Ministry Ideas for The Single Mom. Retrieved from https://www.lifefactors.org/articles/january-ministry-ideas-for-the-single-mom-year

TerKeurst, L. (2018). *It's Not Supposed to Be This Way: Finding Unexpected Strength When Disappointments Leave You Shattered.* Thomas Nelson.
ISBN-10: 0718039858
ISBN-13: 978-0718039851

APPENDIX G

About the Contributors

Leigh "Dangerous Lee" Langston

Leigh Langston is the Publisher at DangerousLee.biz. Dangerous Lee has 13 years' experience writing, editing, and publishing content for the internet.

How The Story of Dangerous Lee Began: The story of Dangerous Lee began with the humor advice column, Ask Dangerous Lee, where she dished out opinions on love, relationships, pop culture, and celebrities.

Ask Dangerous Lee was published monthly in the now-defunct Uncommon Sense newspaper based in Flint, MI and syndicated in various independent magazines and websites nationwide. It can now be read exclusively at DangerousLee.biz.

In 2008, her short erotic story, *Til Death Do Us Part*," was featured in the New York Times Best Selling anthology, *Succulent: Chocolate Flava 2*, edited by Zane.

In March of 2010, Dangerous Lee self-published her first book titled, *Keep Your Panties Up and Your Skirt Down*, an anthology that includes six erotic stories with an emphasis on HIV education. The book is now an Amazon bestseller!

Dangerous Lee also has experience as a certified HIV Prevention Specialist and testing counselor with Wellness AIDS Services, Inc. of Flint, Michigan. Her experience with Wellness helped to shape many of the stories featured in her book.

Ask Dangerous Lee, the column, lead to the Ask Dangerous Lee Live radio show on the Blog Talk Radio network.

For more than two years, Dangerous Lee, along with co-host, hip hop artist, Hassahn Phenomenon, featured celebrities on all sides of the entertainment spectrum.

She was also the co-host of The Radio Happy Hour with Dr. Blogstein, the top comedy show on the Blog Talk Radio network.

Working as a one-woman production, Dangerous Lee has secured more than 100 media features over the course of her career and has taken this website to be ranked in the top 11,000 websites in the U.S. in 2013.

Dangerous Lee has had the pleasure of being selected as Vibe Magazine's Vixen of the Day, as well as being featured on The TODAY Show with Kathie Lee & Hoda!

She has also worked as a contributing writer for actress, Monique Coleman's official website, GimmeMo.com and was the co-founder of Book Bizarre, an event that highlighted self-published authors in Flint, Michigan in 2010 and 2011.

In 2013, The Dangerous Lee Network received 3 million views, was nominated for four Black Weblog Awards, and selected as a Top Fashion Blog to follow in 2013 and 2014.

In October of 2014, Dangerous Lee self-published an eBook based on her highly popular web series, *The Half Series: When Black People Look White*.

In February 2015, The Dangerous Lee Network made a major change to become the #FeedArt Network, a portal for helping independent artists and creative entrepreneurs with their social media marketing efforts.

In 2017, DangerousLee.biz became a business and lifestyle blog catered to the promotion of Black women business owners/entrepreneurs.

Dangerous Lee has taken her years of working on the internet and creating websites and combined it with the experience of marketing herself and other creatives online to work as Everythang in Chief of this website.

In 2021, she opened the Dangerous Lee Mall to provide fashion apparel to women who love clothing and accessories that make a bold statement.

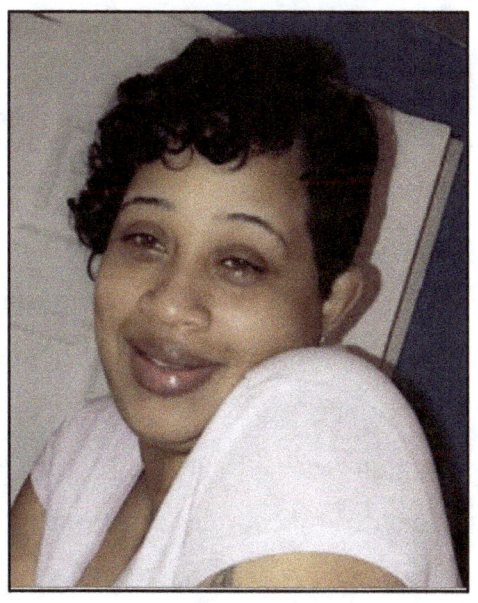

Bianca "BJay" James

Bianca James was born and raised in Flint, MI. She is her mom's only child and the oldest of her dad's three children.

She attended Flint Community Schools, graduating in the class of 2001. BJay works full time as a Nursing Assistant at Hurley Medical Center. She plans to attend University of Michigan Flint in the spring 2022 to earn her Bachelor of Science degree in

Nursing. Her future goal is to become a Registered Nurse (RN).

BJay is a single mother of two teenagers, Yasir and Akeelah. She was raised in a single parent household. Her mother, who was 16 when she gave birth to BJay, was an awesome mother who instilled values and strong work ethnics. Her desire was to always work in the health care field, where she had her hands in many different roles as Direct Care Worker, Med Tech, Dietary Aide, and CAN. She also managed a group home.

Bianca loves to spend time with her children, her extended family and mostly serving the Lord.

Kelcy Williams

Kelcy Williams is the Founder and Executive Director of N Spire U Community Organization. She also serves as CEO and President of N Spire U Productions Inc. Kelcy has been a Playwright/Director for over 20 years. She is also a Screenwriter and Book Author. Some of her work include stage performances: In the Midst of a Storm, Shackled Down, A Generation that Knoweth NOT God, What Would Jesus Do, Un-Shattered Dreams, and others. Kelcy is also the screenwriter and director of short film, Outside That Door, starring her son, B. Jay Williams. In 2020, Kelcy authored and self-published her first book, Un-Dying Love of a Mother (The Odessie Williams Story), an amazing and intriguing story about her mother's life and legacy. She also authored the book, The Shackles of Love, based on her stage performance, Shackled Down. All stories written are INSPIRED by the Holy Spirit and motivated by her desire to uplift and encourage others.

With Kelcy's strong desire and passion for empowering youth to follow their dreams, she founded the annual Talent and Skill Development Camp for Youth; created to help children discover, nurture, and develop their God-given gift/talent. Kelcy is family-oriented and enjoys working on events with her family. She has two sons, B. Jay and Braylen, and her pride and joy - grandson, Blake Jay Williams. In Kelcy's "day" job, she's a Property Analyst in Real Estate, with the State of Michigan/Michigan Department of Transportation.

Varonica Moore

Varonica Moore was born in Sanford, NC. She relocated to Flint MI in the 1950's. Varonica and her 6 siblings were raised by her single mother until her passing when Varonica was 16yrs old. Losing her mom and having her first son at a young age required Varonica to be more responsible and mature for most teenagers her age but hard work and determination kept her on the right path. She graduated from Flint Northwestern High School and had a career in the hospitality field for over 40yrs. She is the single mother of four adult children (3 boys and 1 girl) and grandmother to eleven. Seeing her children become successful adults has been one of her greatest accomplishments.

Sierra Wineman

Sierra Wineman is a single mother from Flint, MI. She has a two-year-old daughter and a five-year-old son.

Sierra have been through a lot in life as a single mother. The responsibility of raising her children was all on her. She credits her children, who are her strength and world, for getting her through each and every day. One of Sierra's biggest accomplishment was graduating from high school. During her senior year, her son was born eight weeks early. As a single mother, she was able to finish high school, while working and supporting her preemie son.

Sierra currently works as a CAN, where she takes care of the elderly. She has continued her education by taking classes through her employer.

This has allowed her to become certified in other areas of her job, which allows her to provide additional services to the elderly. It is Sierra's passion to take care of people. Her ultimate goal is to earn her Bachelor of Science degree in Nursing and become a Registered Nurse (RN).

Sierra drive and motivation is for her children. She is determined to work very hard to give them the life they deserve.

Alexis Rae Brown

Alexis Rae Brown was born in Flint, MI. She is the oldest of six children with two brothers and three sisters. Alexis graduated from Lake-Ville Memorial High School in 2006. She attended Western Michigan University where she was on a four-year Track and Field Scholarship.

Alexis graduated in 2011 with a Bachelor's degree in Aviation Flight Science. She now lives in Atlanta, Georgia with her 10-year-old daughter, Aubrey. As a single mother, she faces the challenges of motherhood and having a full-time job as a First Officer with United Airlines. Growing up, her family showed her the importance of hard work, determination, and perseverance. Thankful for her family's support, she has been able to live out her dream as a Pilot while also caring for her daughter. Her goal and focus in life are to instill, in her daughter, the same morals and values her family instilled in her, by being an example.

Shareatha Brown-Person

Shareatha Brown-Person was born in Flint, MI, where

she graduated from Flint Academy High School. In 1992, Shareatha moved to Indianapolis, IN.

After 14 years working in Corporate America, Shareatha, a single mom decided to start a business from her home. She began her business as Shars Hair, LLC, for the purpose of selling manufactured custom wigs. Originally, the overall driving force behind becoming an entrepreneur stemmed from a medical condition (Alopecia) that caused her to experience hair loss. During that phase of life, she discovered the flexibility and versatility that wigs provided. She began to research and study "cranial prosthesis" and soon became a self-proclaimed "Wigologist". Shars Hair,

LLC soon added boutique items and broadened the name (Dba/ Shars Hair Boutique, 2008). In 2009, one year after opening the business, her mother was diagnosed with stage 3 breast cancer. Her mother was very strong, consistent and determined in her battle with the disease, and is now a breast cancer survivor. It was during this time and journey that Shars Hair, LLC extended the "custom wig/Boutique" business to include a durable medical supply component (Dba/ Shars Medical Supplies). Currently, this division provides garments such as mastectomy bras and prosthesis that meet specific needs of a woman's body after breast cancer surgery. The product line also includes therapeutic shoes and socks to assist clients with neuropathy due to diabetes and other medical conditions. Shar' Medical Supplies, LLC. is one of the only female minority owned DME companies serving Indiana, Ohio and Michigan areas.

Her son attends University of Evansville, Evansville, Indiana. Shareatha married Steven Person on June 23, 2022. She and her husband live in Indianapolis, IN.

Torri J. Gunter

Torri J. Gunter is a native of Flint, MI. She currently resides in Fairburn, Georgia.

Torri is the mother of two amazing children, Meah and Landin. She is a proud graduate of Flint Community Schools and earned a Bachelor's Degree in Sociology from the University of Michigan-Flint in 2011.

Torri is a proud member of Delta Sigma Theta Sorority, Inc. Torri enjoys traveling, spending time with family and diving into new adventures including most recently making a career change from corporate America to logistics. Torri mantra is "It's never too late to start over."

Brandi Allicia Johnson

Brandi Allicia Johnson lives in Clinton, MS. She has been teaching for the last 13 years as a certified teacher. Brandi has a Bachelor's degree in Elementary Education and Master's Degree in Effective Student Leadership. She is the single parent of a 13 years old son. She enjoys creativity activities making t-shirts and home crafts.

Brandi's mantra is "YOUR PERSONAL EXPERIENCES ARE TO HELP OTHERS! FAITH BREAKS ALL CHAINS!!"

Whitney DL Brown

Whitney Brown was born and raised in Flint, Michigan. She graduated from Carman Ainsworth High School (CAHS) in 2014. Whitney attends Baker College and will graduate in May 2022, with her Bachelor's Degree in Criminal Justice. Whitney works full-time at a local high school, as well as, coach the JV and Varsity Cheerleader Teams at CAHS.

Whitney is the mother of two sweet daughters, Nicole (5), and Nyla (3). Whitney loves to travel and do fun kid friendly activities with her daughters. She plans to relocate after graduation, to better their lives as a team.

Kimberley D. Ogburn, M.A. LPCC

Kimberley D. Ogburn is a Licensed Professional Clinical Counselor (LPCC) in the states of Ohio and Maryland.

    She has a Master's Degree in Counseling from the University of Akron and a Bachelor's Degree in Social Work from Cleveland State University. She is skilled in the areas of Cognitive Behavioral Therapy, Trauma-Focused Cognitive Behavioral Therapy for

Children, Brief Counseling and Crisis Intervention and Mediation.

Two years ago, Kimberley's husband (Andre) of six years, passed away unexpectedly, thrusting her into the role of single parenthood and having to rely on the coping mechanisms she counsels her clients in for herself and for her children.

Reva Caughel Winningham

Reva Caughel Winningham was raised in Otisville, Michigan. She is a graduate of Lakeville High School, Class of 1975. She continued her studies at Kee Business College, where she graduated in 1985 with a degree in Accounting.

Michell Berkley

Michell Berkley was born in the early '80s in Saginaw, Michigan and was raised in Flint, Michigan. Her mother, who divorced from her father at a young age, raised her and her brother alone with plenty of support and love from family. Michell attended the Carmen Ainsworth Schools and received her GED from Flint Zimmerman Center. She graduated from Ross Medical School with a Certification in Medical Administration & Billing. She is currently working for Instacart Corp. Michell is a single mother to two beautiful daughters. She became a proud homeowner in 2016. Michell is a member of Victorious Word Church, where Rev. Rodney Murphy is the Pastor. Michell enjoys spending time with her daughters, family members and close friends.

Dr. Dawn Demps

Dr. Dawn Demps is a Flint, MI native that has been involved with community advocacy and organizing since she was 12 years old. She utilizes her own lived experiences to connect with students and parents to promote tools for self-advocacy, structural reforms and strives to champion the concerns of these populations.

Dawn developed her own youth initiative called Eyes on the Prize (EOTP) that used the fine arts to reach out to resources denied young people in urban communities to help them reach their full potential academically, emotionally, and creatively. Over 10 years, EOTP served over 2500 at-promise youth. Eight years after dropping out of high school, Dawn entered a community college and continued on to complete her studies at the University of Michigan-Flint as a double major in Africana Studies and Social Sciences.

Dawn served as the Executive Director of Leadership Development In Interethnic Relations (LDIR), an organization dedicated to nurturing citizen leaders equipped to navigate the complexities of -isms that separate individuals in an effort to build strong intergroup collaborations. She was Director of Youth, Education and Community Projects for the Urban League of Flint and served nearly 400 youth and families every year through afterschool and summer programs, parent workshops and community advocacy trainings. She was the Executive Director of the Urban Center for Post-Secondary Access and Success (UPASS) which helped students successfully navigate high school and tackle postsecondary challenges and opportunities. Through her long history of community work, Dawn has had the privilege of working with nationally renowned scholars and innovators such as: educational sociologist, Dr. Pedro Noguera, environmental justice crusader, Majora Carter, Dr. Tyrone Howard, UCLA educator and author and non-violence advocate and Hip-Hop legend KRS-One.

Dawn holds an MA in Social Justice Studies from Marygrove College in Detroit, MI and received her Ph.D. from Arizona State University in Education Policy and Evaluation. Her dissertation was a critical ethnographic oral history study of a grassroots community advocacy group comprised of Black natural and other mothers whom galvanized to challenge and dismantle the educational policies and practices that exclude Black children from educational spaces. She has published articles examining the possibilities of youth inspired school leadership as exhibited through youth voice and participatory action research, unpacking the difficulties and potential of

Black and Brown collaborative educational leadership and how art can be used to expose the experiences of Black youth who have experienced school exclusion. She is currently an Assistant Professor at the University of Arizona's College of Education in Education Policy Studies and Practice.

Dawn has been awarded the 2020/21 American Association of University Women Dissertation Fellowship and Arizona State University Dissertation Completion Fellowship. A sample of her other recognitions include the 2019 University Council for Education Administration (UCEA) Putting Research Into Action Award, 2019 Hilliard Sizemore Research Fellow, UCEA Barbara Jackson Scholar and Ford Foundation Pre-Doctoral Fellowship Honorable Mention. She additionally serves as a member of the Arizona Department of Education's African American Advisory Council and is the proud mother of 3 children: Journi, Jayanti and Zora - ages 19, 17 and 9 respectively.

She can be followed at www.dawndemps.com and @dawndemps

APPENDIX H

About the Author

Dr. Brenda Brown

Dr. Brenda Brown is a single mother of three and grandmother of seven. She is a twin and one of 13 children born to Jim and Marchel Brown. Her willingness to serve and to help people is captured even in her career goal to "help students to succeed and be prepared for the economic and social opportunities that will empower them as individuals." She practices what she preaches. Her parents instilled in Brenda and her siblings the importance of education. Though she encountered many hurdles – including racial, social, and economic – she persevered, earning an associate, bachelor's, master's, and then doctoral degree. She held the same high expectations for her children, whom she inspired to achieve higher education degrees. Brenda carries a can-do spirit as she guides and encourages others, regardless of their circumstances, to grow and learn. Her mantra is a Nelson Mandela quote: "An education is the most powerful weapon which you can use to change the world."

Beyond home and work, she believes that giving back is vital to promoting community – and she does! Her past volunteer efforts include Big Brothers Big Sisters of Greater Flint (BB/BS), the Beecher Scholarship Incentive Program, the Genesee County Reaching Across the Nation Consortium, Department of Human Services Michigan Youth Opportunity Initiatives, the Gateway Cultivating Our Community garden project, and the United Way. Perhaps most notable, for over 30 years, Brenda has served as a mentor for BB/BS. She also mentored for Living Independently Networking Knowledge (L.I.N.K.), volunteered as the coordinator for her church's weekly A Taste of Tutoring program, and served as the Amachi liaison between BB/BS and her church. She has been a past mentor for West Bendle and Garfield Elementary Schools' Help One Student To Succeed (HOSTS) programs (6 years), an advisor to the Baker College Tutoring Association's tutoring programs for Flint Community Schools and Bendle Public Schools (15 years), and a former co-chair of Flint Area Citizens to End Racism Youth Action Team and Steering Committee (5 years). She has served as facilitator of the Great Lakes District Youth Leadership (1 year) and board member of Flint Leadership Development in Interethnic Relations (2 years). She also served as a member of the Flint Area Public Affairs Forum (1 year).

Her current volunteer positions include co-chair of the Genesee Intermediate School District (GISD) Parent Advisory Council, member of GISD

Parent Café, and member of the Dr. Martin Luther King Jr. Tribute Dinner Planning Committee.

In all her community service, Brenda brings courage, commitment, compassion, and understanding that have continued to grow from her early childhood experiences as being part of the only minority family in a small, rural community. Befriended by one White, female classmate, following high school graduation, Brenda was determined to similarly become a champion for social justice. Her faith serves as a strong foundation. She is an active member of Prince of Peace Missionary Baptist Church, where she is a Sunday school teacher and serves in multiple ministries.

Brenda lives, works, and volunteers – demonstrating the essence of Luke 12:48 (KJV), "For unto whomsoever much is given, of him shall be much required: and to whom men have committed much, of him they will ask the more."

Brenda worked as an administrator and adjunct faculty before retiring from Baker College after 27 years of service in 2019.

In her spare time, Brenda enjoys spending time with her children and grandchildren.

Brenda is the author of *The Day I Forgot But Will Always Remember (Living With Sudden Cardiac Arrest)*, and co-author of *Prayer Can Change Everything*.

Media Articles

https://www.abc12.com/content/news/Newsmaker-for-the-week-of-February-16-2020--567985941.html

https://www.abc12.com/content/news/Back-from-illness-Crim-racer-gets-2nd-chance-to-cross-finish-line-399937091.html

https://www.abc12.com/content/news/Newsmaker-Two-authors-discuss-their-new-inspirational-books-about-defying-the-odds-510473311.html

https://www.flintside.com/features/brendabrown.aspx

https://www.flintside.com/features/Q-%20A-with-authro-Brenda-Brown-who-died-and-lived-to-tell-the-tale.aspx

Social Media

https://www.youtube.com/channel/UCKXvM3XT0Lj5m_L_564WGMA

@bbrown9836

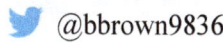
@bbrown9836

Books by Dr. Brenda Brown

The Day I Forgot - But Will Always Remember (Living With Sudden Cardiac Arrest)

The Day I Forgot - But Will Always Remember relates the story of a woman who suffered sudden cardiac arrest (SCA) while walking in a 10-mile road race. Readers are given an inside look at her struggle with posttraumatic stress, cognitive challenges, and adjusting to her new reality.

This book raises awareness of a hidden, often-deadly heart condition. It provides survivors and survivors' family and friends with a better understanding and mindfulness of the challenges SCA survivors deal with daily. Included are stories from other SCA survivors, from across the county, who share the difficult aspects of their encounter with death and of reentering this life. Frequently asked questions, case studies, articles, and resources that can equip the bystanders on how to administer immediate treatment with CPR, or an automated external defibrillator (AED) to give the victim the best chance at life is also included.

ISBN-10: 057849342X
ISBN-13: 978-0578493428

Prayer Can Change Everything

Prayer is an essential spiritual practice that helps to build and strengthen our relationship and faith in God. Through these intentional conversations with the creator, we express our gratitude, give praise, and make our requests known. In the inspiring anthology, Prayer Can Change Everything, Telishia Berry presents 29 empowering coauthors who share affirmations, poems, prayers, and stories to uplift, encourage, and empower you.

Prayer Can Change Everything is not an ordinary book. In it, you will find poignant and meditative reads that will elevate your thoughts and soothe your soul. Once you have been stirred by the power of this meaningful work, please don't hesitate to share it to allow others to experience its full purpose.

ISBN-10: 0978600193
ISBN-13: 978-0978600198

Single Mothers Syndrome – By Choice or By Design (An Open Dialogue)

There is this persistent thoughts or beliefs that single mothers are separate from most of society. These thoughts and beliefs lead some single mothers to give up and use single parenting as an excuse, or justification, or as a reason to hold themselves back. This book provides readers with a better understanding and mindfulness of the challenge single mothers deal with daily. Included are the conversations from 15 single mothers, from across the country, who share their journey in hopes of inspiring, motivating, and provoking objective thought on single motherhood.

ISBN: 978-0-578-35349-4
ISBN: 978-0-578-35350-0

Notes

Meet the Author & Contributors
May 7, 2022, at 6:30 PM EST
Via Zoom

Register at: http://evite.me/epTVHScR9Z

Email the author at drbrendabrown9836@gmail.com

www.ingramcontent.com/pod-product-compliance
Lightning Source LLC
Chambersburg PA
CBHW051427290426
44109CB00016B/1466